SHIPS OF THE
U S NAVY

SHIPS OF THE
U S NAVY

Exeter Books

NEW YORK

A Bison Book

CONTENTS

Introduction	6
The US Navy Today	11
Aircraft and Weapons of the Fleet	43
Strategic Missile Submarines	77
Attack Submarines	85
Aircraft Carriers	97
Battleships	111
Cruisers	117
Destroyers	129
Frigates	139
Amphibious Ships, Craft and Vehicles	149
Patrol Ships and Craft	163
Mine Countermeasures Ships and Craft	169
Support Ships	175
Afterword	185
Glossary	188
Index	189

First published in USA 1987
by Exeter Books
Distributed by Bookthrift
Exeter is a trademark of Bookthrift
Marketing, Inc.
Bookthrist is a registered trademark of
Bookthrift Marketing,
New York, New York

ISBN 0-671-08913-7

Printed in Hong Kong

PAGE 1: *The veteran battleship
BB61* Iowa *launches a Harpoon
antiship missile*

PAGES 2-3: *CGN 25* Bainbridge,
*one of the nine US nuclear-
powered missile cruisers.*

BELOW: *The* Adams *class missile
destroyer DDG 17* Conyngham.

INTRODUCTION

How strong is the United States Navy today?

That it *should* be the strongest navy in the world is something that most Americans now take for granted, although in what ways and at what cost are subjects of seemingly inexhaustible debate. Yet perhaps it is worth remembering that neither the expectation nor the possibility of US naval supremacy has had a very long history.

When the American Navy was informally born in 1775 the British Navy was capable of deploying at least 100 battleships (*ie*, ships of 74 to 120 guns) and a much larger number of frigates (28-38 guns). At best, the Continental Navy was never able to deploy more than 20 frigate-sized ships to oppose this mighty force. Nor after 1798, when the US Navy Department was officially created, did matters rapidly improve. The US Navy had but 16 seagoing vessels (seven frigates, four corvettes and five lighter craft) when the nation again went to war with Great Britain in 1812. By 1861 the Navy still had only about 90 vessels of all sorts, most of them obsolete by European standards. To be sure, under pressure of the Civil War this figure soared to 670 by 1865, and for a brief time the US Navy was the world's largest; but it was still far from being the world's strongest, since many of its ships (such as shallow-water monitors and paddle-wheel riverboats) were too specialized to be able to take an effective part in any international naval war.

Throughout most of the remainder of the nineteenth century the US remained well down on the list of leading naval powers, and only in 1905 did it briefly achieve second place, a position it soon lost when the great pre-World War I European naval armaments race began. Although by the 1920s it was evident that US industrial might now made it *possible* for America to deploy the world's most powerful navy, this was a possibility the nation declined, preferring instead to put its faith in naval arms-limitation treaties. When the advent of World War II swept away the last vestiges of these already bankrupt treaties, the US Navy was still less powerful than Britain's Royal Navy and arguably no stronger than the Imperial Japanese Navy.

Thus it was only a little over 40 years ago, probably sometime in 1943, that America became for the first time the world's premier naval power. But when this happened, it happened overwhelmingly. By January 1944 there were over

RIGHT: *The Atlantic Fleet puts to sea from Key West in 1898 to blockade Cuba.*
BELOW: *The frigate* Constitution, *America's most famous warship, is still formally in commission.*

4100 vessels in the US fleet, and by the end of that year the Navy was able to deploy more carriers in a single task force than existed in all the rest of the world combined.

Although America emerged from World War II by far the world's greatest naval power, there were many who felt that the advent of atomic weaponry had made all naval power, as traditionally conceived, a thing of the past. Thus when, in 1948, Congress appropriated funds for the Navy to build a carrier large enough to accommodate atomic bomb-carrying aircraft, critics of seapower (mainly in the Air Force) protested so loudly that Secretary of Defense Louis Johnson cancelled the project. The controversy was only resolved – or, at any rate, muted – in the early 1950s, when the Navy's stellar performance in the Korean war silenced the doubters. The keel of the new carrier – the first of 12 that would be built between then and 1990 – was laid down in 1952.

The vast accumulation of matériel left over from World War II guaranteed that the Navy would remain – if only for want of serious competitors – numerically supreme for at least the first two post-war decades. It was, in fact, still able to deploy nearly 1000 ships in the Vietnam War. But as obsolescence overtook the World War II vessels, and as post-Vietnam anti-militarist sentiment decimated defense budgets in the 1970s, the Navy fell into a precipitous decline. By 1980 it had only about 470 ships left in commission. It was so short of weapons, munitions, fuel and spare parts that no more than 40 percent of its carrier fleet could be deployed at full readiness at any one time. And it was having such recruitment difficulties that 13 percent of all its ships and 25 percent of its aviation squadrons were considered not combat ready because of personnel shortages.

This is not to say that the US Navy of 1980 was demonstrably inferior to its new rival, the rapidly-growing Soviet Navy, but its ascendance was certainly no longer clear cut. Nor was this ambiguity just the result of the Navy's quantitative decline. Military technology was by this time evolving at such a pace that no one could be absolutely certain which of the new weapons, or the tactics and strategies they seemed to call for, would prevail in either a conventional or a nuclear war.

In 1981 President Reagan and his energetic Navy Secretary, John F Lehman, Jr, embarked on an ambitious program to rebuild the Navy. Their quantitative target, 600 ships by the

LEFT: *The old battleship BB 42 Idaho in World War II.*

ABOVE: *Former Secretary of the Navy John F Lehman, Jr.*

end of 1990, was impressive enough, but it was on qualitative improvement that they pinned their real hopes for a return to undisputed naval superiority. And despite mounting opposition from the deficit-conscious Congress, it was clear by the second half of the 1980s that most of the specific goals of this $1 trillion naval program would be realized – a 600-ship fleet that would include 15 carrier battle groups, four battleship-centered surface action groups, many sophisticated new surface combatants, about 100 nuclear-powered attack submarines, over 6000 aircraft and much else.

Will this revitalized fleet confer – has it, in fact, already conferred – the decisive naval superiority sought by the Administration? There is no single or simple answer to such a question, and short of trial by war, perhaps there never can be. But there can of course be some good guesses. The object of this book is to provide the non-specialist reader with as much information as possible to help him make his own good guesses.

Chapter 1
THE US NAVY TODAY

The symbol of US naval might since World War II has been the carrier. Here, CV 66 America beneath planes of her Air Wing.

One way – and no doubt the best single way – to assess the strength of a fleet is to think of it as the aggregate of the strengths of all the individual ships and crews that compose it. But that is still less than the whole story. The capabilities of individual ships can be considerably affected by circumstances external to themselves: the strategic and tactical doctrines that govern how they are to be used, the composition of the particular fleet units in which they find themselves, the specific nature of the opposition they must face and so on.

If this has always been true, it is very much more so today. Now warships are no longer all-purpose. Each is a specialist, capable of addressing only a part of the whole spectrum of naval combat, and each is therefore dependent on other types of ships to supply the capabilities it lacks. And in any case, how good a given ship may be at its specialty at any point in time is always at the mercy of fulminating technologies.

In this chapter we shall touch briefly on some of the external circumstances that help to determine how well the ships of the US Navy may be able to perform their assigned duties in time of war.

Missions and Capabilities

In the broadest sense, the Navy has always had two classic missions: to project the power of the United States up to the coastlines (and, if need be, into the territories) of potential enemies and to guarantee America's control of the seas. Before World War II the first mission, power projection, was generally the less important of the two, being confined mostly to a certain capacity to conduct shore bombardment and limited amphibious operations. But the rise of carrier-borne air power and the enormous increase in amphibious capabilities that occurred during the war sharply increased the Navy's role as a power-projector, and the subsequent advent of nuclear weapons and long-range missiles increased it still more. Indeed, one facet of the Navy's ability to project power has now become so awesome that it is

considered to entail a mission separate from all others. That facet is its capacity to launch enough nuclear missiles to wipe any enemy's country from the face of the earth, and the new mission is (mankind may devoutly hope) the deterrence of nuclear war.

At present the Navy's 'leg' of the triad of American strategic nuclear forces consists primarily in its fleet of 35-40 nuclear-powered ballistic missile submarines (SSBNs), a force capable of launching a total of over 5700 independently targetable warheads, each ranging in explosive yield from the equivalent of 40,000 to 100,000 tons of TNT (40-100 KT). Many analysts consider this submarine force the most formidable leg of the triad, both because the hard-to-detect boats are thought to be less susceptible to surprise attack than land-based missile platforms and because the ballistic missiles they fire are harder to intercept than either manned bombers or cruise missiles.

Yet missile-launching submarines have always been in some degree vulnerable to advances in antisubmarine warfare. By the late 1950s it was clear that only nuclear-powered boats, which could remain submerged for great lengths of time and could fire their missiles from beneath the surface, stood much chance of avoiding destruction in any environment dominated by enemy antisubmarine surface ships and aircraft. Since then the antisubmarine threat has grown so steadily that both the US and Soviet navies now give high priority to the development of submarine-launched missiles with sufficient range to permit the SSBNs to fire them from positions as close as possible to the relative security of home waters. (The Trident D-5 missile, due to be deployed on American SSBNs in the early 1990s, will have a range of about 6000 nautical miles, a 30 percent increase over the range of the present Trident C-4.) But even when operating in 'friendly' waters, SSBNs may still be exposed to assaults from enemy nuclear-powered attack submarines (SSNs), perhaps the most dangerous antisubmarine weapons of all. Thus the SSBNs are by no means invulnerable, and whether future advances in SSBN design can keep pace with advances in antisubmarine warfare is a critical unknown.

So much attention has been paid to SSBNs that it is easy to forget that they do not represent the Navy's only option for delivery of nuclear weapons. Naval aircraft have always had a

LEFT: *A submarine-launched C-4 Trident long-range ballistic missile roars up out of the sea.*
ABOVE: *An American SSBN with its missile hatches open.*
RIGHT: *A technician sits before a console in the missile fire-control room of an* Ohio *class nuclear SSBN.*

tactical delivery capacity, and as of the second half of the 1980s a formidable new delivery vehicle has begun to enter the Navy's arsenal. This is the Tomahawk cruise missile, some 4000 of which have so far been ordered. The Tomahawk can be launched from virtually any fair-sized surface vessel or submarine (it can be launched underwater), and it is currently scheduled for deployment on seven classes of surface ships and five classes of attack submarines. It is potentially launchable from aircraft as well. There are several types of Tomahawk, but in its tactical nuclear version it is said to have a range of about 1350 nm and a warhead yield of 200 KT. Tomahawks are both slower than ballistic missiles and probably somewhat easier to intercept, and they are therefore not ideally suited for instant retaliation. But such large numbers of them could be fired from such a variety of widely dispersed launch platforms that it would be extremely difficult for an enemy to suppress most of them before they could be launched. Once in flight, they might well be able to saturate an enemy's air defense system, especially if it had already been battered by ballistic missiles.

It is worth pointing out here that in the jargon of arms limitations negotiators the sole distinction between 'tactical' and 'strategic' nuclear weapons systems is range. The former are supposed to have ranges only up to 3400 nm, while the latter may have any greater range. Since both carrier-launched bombers and Tomahawks are deemed to have ranges of less than 3400 nm, they are classed as tactical delivery systems. But this does not take into account the mobility of the naval platforms from which they can be launched. It is one thing to be able to launch tactical nuclear missiles against the Soviet Union from relatively fixed bases in Western Europe, and quite another to be able to launch nuclear carrier strikes or Tomahawks from a variety of positions around the Soviet littoral. For example, Tomahawks fired from the Barents Sea and the Sea of Marmara alone could blanket European Russia all the way to the Urals. Thus the peculiar nature of sea power blurs both the definitions and the implications of the terms 'tactical' and 'strategic.'

The Navy's ability to project power in the form of submarine-launched nuclear ballistic missiles – and, to a more limited extent, in the form of sea-to-ground nuclear air strikes and cruise missiles – is a thing apart, related to lesser

TOP: *A Tomahawk cruise missile in flight photographed from a chase plane.*
LEFT: *The airburst of a 1000-lb conventional warhead delivered by a Tomahawk missile.*
RIGHT: *The class leader of the newest and largest class of US carriers, CVN 68* Nimitz.

An EA-6B Prowler, a derivative of the A-6 Intruder and specializing in electronics warfare.

kinds of war and threat only in that it exists to keep them (if possible) from getting out of hand. For less drastic types of power projection, from peacetime crisis management all the way up to 'surgical' nuclear strikes on enemy ships and ports, the Navy continues to rely primarily on the aircraft carrier.

By the early 1990s the Navy hopes to be able to deploy 15 carrier Battle Groups centered on seven nuclear-powered and eight conventionally-powered large carriers, each with a complement of about 80-90 aircraft. At present carrier air wings normally consist of two squadrons of fighters (F-14 Tomcats), two of light attack aircraft (A-7 Corsairs or F/A-18 Hornets), one of medium attack aircraft (A-6 Intruders) and one of antisubmarine aircraft (S-3 Vikings), plus smaller squadrons or detachments of aircraft and helicopters that specialize in various phases of electronic warfare and intelligence gathering, air-early-warning and antisubmarine operations.

Although carrier admirals have traditionally preferred to

stress the power-projection role of aircraft carriers (doubtless for p r reasons vis-a-vis Congressional budget committees), it is clear from the composition of the standard carrier air wing that a Battle Group's planes are equally a potent instrument of sea control and a vital part of the Group's ability to defend itself against air and submarine attack. Accordingly, since 1975, US fleet carriers have no longer been designated CVAs (or 'Attack Carriers'), but simply CVs, a tacit recognition of their multi-purpose role.

For power projection, carrier air wings continue to rely mainly on the deep-strike capabilities of their A-6 Intruders, with the new F/A-18 Hornets rapidly replacing the older A-7 Corsairs as supplementary strike aircraft. The Intruder, with its 450-nm combat radius (considerably extendable via inflight refueling), its all-weather capabilities and its munitions-carrying capacity second only to that of an Air Force four-engine B-52, is in many ways an impressive aircraft. It can launch several types of air-to-surface standoff weapons

The newest combat aircraft in the Navy's inventory, the F/A-18 Hornet fighterbomber.

already – Maverick, Harpoon and HARM – and is potentially capable of launching Tomahawks. But it is elderly – over 25 years old – and subsonic. The Navy has performed prodigies in progressively up-grading this stalwart with hi-tech retrofittings, and it will doubtless remain the backbone of the carrier air wings' deep-strike ability well into the 1990s. But of course it will eventually have to be replaced. In 1986, for the first time, the Navy and the Air Force agreed to cooperate in the development of the next generation of attack (and also fighter) aircraft for both services, but how productive this cooperation will prove to be, or how it may be affected by future defense budgets, is anyone's guess.

The Hornet was originally seen less as a replacement for the Intruder than as a supplement to it – just as it was also intended as a supplement to the Navy's standard fighter, the F-14 Tomcat. When the dual-purpose Hornet was first introduced early in the 1980s it was the subject of much controversy. Critics said that it was a jack of two trades and the master of neither, but in service it has proven to be a better plane than even its partisans predicted. As an attack plane (it can shift from an attack mode to a fighter mode simply with the flick of a switch), it has somewhat less range than the Intruder and lacks the Intruder's all-weather abilities, but it is twice as fast and can carry nearly the same weight of munitions. If there is no replacement for the Intruder before the end of the century, the Hornet will perforce assume more and more of its responsibilities. As of the latter part of the 1980s Hornets were entering service at the rate of about 150 per year, and the Navy's total procurement plans for the type exceeded 1300 units.

In addition to submarine-launched ICBMs, cruise missiles and carrier-borne attack aircraft, the Navy disposes of another major instrument of power-projection: its amphibious forces. At the end of World War II many people thought that amphibious warfare was probably a thing of the past. In 1949 no less an authority than General Omar Bradley could say, 'I predict that large-scale amphibious operations will never occur again.' The timing was perhaps unfortunate, for within a year General Douglas MacArthur would conduct one of the most daring and decisive amphibious operations in history at Inchon, Korea.

Nevertheless, in terms of specialist ships in commission,

the Navy's amphibious fleet declined steadily. It had had some 3000 amphibious ships and craft at the end of World War II, a force that had dwindled to about 200 during the Korean War and around 160 at the height of the Vietnam War. By the mid-1980s the amphibious fleet consisted of only about 60 ships in active service, with approximately another 30 that could be allocated to some form of amphibious duties in an emergency.

Yet numbers alone are not the whole story, for many of these modern ships are extremely sophisticated and capable, reflective of the ways in which amphibious tactics themselves have changed in the years since World War II. This 60-ship fleet, in fact, is theoretically capable of lifting the assault echelon of one 48,000-man Marine Amphibious Force, along with its air wing and its essential support elements. By 1996 the Navy plans to expand this force to a core of about 75 ships, so that it will be able to service an additional 15,000-man Marine Amphibious Brigade and its air group.

ABOVE: *The amphibious assault helicopter carrier LPH 9* Guam *anchored off Genoa.*
RIGHT: *The most advanced types of amphibious ships in service now are the LHAs of the* Tarawa *class, soon to be surpassed by the new* Wasp *LHDs.*

What makes it possible to deploy such numbers of troops on so few bottoms is the advent of new technologies in amphibious warfare. In World War II it was necessary for troop transports to come relatively close inshore, and then for the assault troops to be ferried to the beaches in a variety of special landing ships and craft that formed part of the invasion fleet. By the 1950s, however, it became apparent that much of the ferrying job could be performed more quickly and efficiently by helicopters in a form of initial assault that came to be called 'vertical envelopment.' This had the added advantage of permitting the transports to conduct the initial assault from much farther offshore – from over the horizon, in fact. But since the load-carrying capacity of helicopters was limited, heavy equipment and reinforcements still had to be brought to the beaches by sea. What was therefore needed to confer a true over-the-horizon amphibious capability was both bigger and more capacious helicopters, some new form of high-speed, long-range landing craft and transport ships capable of accomodating both.

By the mid-1980s the Navy had gone a long way towards meeting all these requirements. The standard CH-46 Sea Knight helicopter can transport 18 fully-armed troops, and its new, larger cousin, the CH-53E Super Stallion, 56. To supplement conventional LCU and LCM landing craft, a radical new type of air-cushion landing craft, the LCAC, is beginning to enter service. The LCACs can carry 60-75 tons of cargo (including an M60 tank) or 250 Marines for distances of up to 200 nm at an incredible speed of 40-50 knots, and they can land on an estimated 70 percent of the world's beaches, as opposed to the 17 percent available to conventional landing craft. A force of highly specialized transport ships resembling small aircraft carriers has been developed to bring troops, helicopters and LCACs or conventional landing craft within range of their targets. The newest of these ships, those of the *Wasp* class, entering service in the late 1980s, can carry over 2000 troops, the equivalent of 32 CH-46s and three LCACs, as well as six Marine vertical-or-short-take-off-and-land Harrier attack aircraft (the same plane that performed so well for the Royal Navy in the Falklands fighting). The airlift capacity of these ships may be further enhanced in the 1990s by the advent of a new tilt-rotor airplane, the MV-22 Osprey, that can carry about the same loads as present-day helicopters over

considerably longer ranges at twice the speed.

The carrier-like *Wasps*, *Tarawas* and *Iwo Jimas* are only the cutting edge of the Navy's amphibious fleet. Other ship types include the more conventional (though now much-improved) attack cargo ships, landing ship docks, tank landing ships and such like first developed in World War II.

Not strictly part of the Navy's amphibious forces, but certainly an important element in its ability to project power, is the Maritime Prepositioning Force, one feature of the Rapid Deployment strategy developed by the Carter Administration in the wake of the Iranian hostage crisis of the late 1970s. The MPF is not technically an amphibious force because, as it is presently set up, it requires a certain minimum of 'friendly' port facilities to off-load the troops and matériel it can carry. But given that limitation, it can nevertheless move out very rapidly from its permanent forward bases in response to

ABOVE: *The interior of a CH-46 Sea Knight helicopter. It can carry up to 18 fully equipped Marine troops.*
LEFT: *'Jeff B,' test prototype of the radical new air-cushion LCAC landing craft.*

fast-breaking crises. The MPF now consists of three squadrons: one prepositioned in the Eastern Atlantic, one in the Indian Ocean and one in the Western Pacific. Each MPS consists of four or five ships (either new constructions or extensively modified merchant vessels) with more than enough capacity to support the approximately 15,000 men of a Marine Amphibious Brigade for 30 days. The rapid-response capabilities of the MPF are thus fairly impressive, but in what scenarios it might be needed is difficult to predict.

The Navy has one final power-projection instrumentality, perhaps the most controversial of the whole array. Beginning in 1982 reactivated and extensively refitted World War II-type *Iowa* class battleships began to come back into service in the fleet. By the 1990s four of these old monsters will be on active duty, each to form the centerpiece of a task force called a Surface Action Group. Because the *Iowas* retain their original main batteries of nine 16-inch guns (each gun capable of hurling a one-ton shell nearly 25 miles), they dispose of by far the heaviest traditional naval ordnance anywhere afloat. In addition, the first two units of the class, *New Jersey* and *Iowa*, have been fitted to carry 32 Tomahawk cruise missiles and 16 Harpoon ship-to-ship missiles. Presumably, the remaining two units, *Missouri* and *Wisconsin*, will be no less heavily armed when they put to sea late in the 1980s.

Like carriers, the battleships can be used both for power projection and sea control. In the former role, acting either in support of amphibious operations or independently, they can use their big guns to bombard shore installations, and they can fire their Tomahawks at other targets hundreds of miles inland. Plainly they would also be formidable opponents in surface combat at sea, though whether their particular mix of weapons would give them any special advantage over modern guided missile cruisers and destroyers is unclear. Critics have argued that the *Iowas'* big guns are not really very relevant to modern warfare in general or to sea fighting in particular and that as missile platforms the ships are not only needlessly ponderous and expensive but are inviting targets. Advocates point to the sheer volume of firepower the battleships command and insist that their massive armor plating makes them better able to survive battle damage than any other warships now at sea. The truth of any of these pros and cons remains to be demonstrated.

Battleships and aircraft carriers are obviously both power projectors and sea-control vessels, but in fact virtually all power-projection ships have at least some ability to fight at sea. For example, all American strategic submarines carry, in addition to their missiles, long-range wire-guided Mk 48 torpedoes that can be fired at surface ships or other submarines; and amphibious assault ships such as those of the *Wasp* class can be converted into true miniature aircraft carriers simply by replacing their troop-transport helicopters with Harrier attack aircraft. (The *Wasps* can, in their carrier mode, embark 20 Harriers, as well as four antisubmarine helicopters).

But except for carriers and battleships, most major sea-control ships are in some degree specialist. All of them are specially designed to fight sea battles both offensively and defensively, albeit in varying degrees and in different ways. As a result, it is difficult to say which one type is the most potent, but certainly the nuclear-powered attack submarine, the SSN, yields pride of place to none.

ABOVE: *A Maritime Prepositioning ship,* Second Lt John H Bobo *in the Indian Ocean.*
RIGHT: *BB 61* Iowa *practice fires her massive 16-in main battery.*

When the world's first SSN, USS *Nautilus*, was launched in 1954 most people still thought that its principal wartime targets would be surface ships. But the advent of ballistic missile submarines changed all that, and since the 1960s the primary mission of SSNs has been to destroy enemy submarines. As of the mid-1980s America's foremost attack submarines were those of the *Los Angeles* class. Although Soviet *Alfa* SSNs can both travel faster under water and dive almost twice as deep, the *Los Angeles* boats are still generally held to be the finest ASW (antisubmarine warfare) platforms now afloat, this because of their quietness and reliability and the extreme sophistication of their sensors, computers and weaponry. They can carry up to about 25 Mk 48 torpedoes, or any one of several combinations of torpedoes, SUBROC antisubmarine rockets, Tomahawk cruise missiles, Harpoon antiship missiles, mines and so on – all of which can be launched under water. It is said that virtually no Soviet SSBN ever enters the Atlantic without being shadowed so closely by one or more US SSNs that the sound of the Russian missile hatches opening would be audible to the Americans. Perhaps significantly, no such claims have yet been made for either the Pacific or Indian Oceans.

ABOVE: *SSN 571* Nautilus *was the world's first nuclear-powered ship.*
OPPOSITE: *An antisubmarine ASROC rocket fired from the guided missile cruiser CG 21* Gridley.
RIGHT: *A chart showing the growth in size of US submarines since the turn of the century.*
FAR RIGHT: *An artist's impression of the proposed SSN 21* Seawolf.

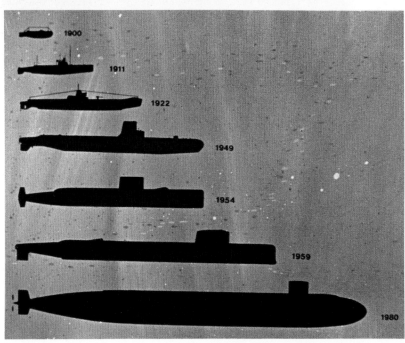

By 1986 submarine/antisubmarine warfare had come to be regarded by many strategists as the Navy's top priority, and an elaborate study known as 'The Antisubmarine Master Plan and Investment Strategy' was undertaken. Details of the study's conclusions are secret, but it is known to include recommendations for the rapid construction of a new class of SSNs, the *Seawolfs*, that will represent a major technical advance over the already-formidable *Los Angeles* boats. The first *Seawolf* is due to join the fleet in 1995, at which time the Navy will have about 100 SSNs of all types on active duty. By then their armament may be augmented with a new type of stand-off antisubmarine rocket now under development, the Sea Lance, with a range much greater than that of SUBROC.

Destroying enemy submarines may be the SSNs' primary mission, but plainly they are a daunting threat to all surface ships as well. SSNs can attack surface ships with tactically configured Tomahawks from a distance of 250 nm, with Harpoons from 60 nm and with torpedoes from about 20 nm. (And, of course, with strategically configured Tomahawks they can also strike at land targets over 1300 nm away.) There is much warrant, therefore, for those who argue that SSNs are the most powerful of all sea control vessels.

Can the SSNs be successfully countered by anything but other SSNs – or indeed, can they be countered at all? They are not too difficult to destroy; the problem is to locate them. To this end the Navy has strewn the oceans' floors with listening devices – the so-called Sound Surveillance System (SOSUS) – and has deployed both sophisticated satellites equipped with visual and infrared sensors and ASW patrol aircraft that can monitor the oceans' surfaces and probe its depths with sono-buoys. To abet conventional ship- and submarine-borne sonars ultra-sensitive Towed Array Sonar Systems can be streamed up to three miles behind ships and submarines. And on the drawing boards are exotic new sensor systems based on lasers, magnetic detectors and synthetic aperture radars. Yet all the while submarines get quieter, dive deeper and become ever harder to detect.

In Battle and Surface Action Groups all the principal escort ships – cruisers, destroyers and frigates – carry ASW sensors and weapons. The two main ship-launched weapons are the lightweight Mk 46 homing torpedo and ASROC, a rocket that can project a Mk 46 or a nuclear depth charge a distance of

about 6 nm. Since the range of the Mk 46 itself is less than 5 nm, even when assisted by ASROC it is still a short-range weapon. To give it the reach it would almost certainly need in all but last-ditch battle conditions it must therefore be air-launched. To this end, many surface escort types, as well as carriers and battleships, carry ASW helicopters capable of launching Mk 46s anywhere in a considerable radius from the center of a task force. The most advanced of these helicopters, the SH-60B Seahawk, can 'loiter' for an hour over patches of ocean up to 150 nm distant from its launch pad. Its advanced ASW system, called LAMPS-III, includes sophis-

ticated radars, sonobuoys, magnetic anomaly detectors and computers, as well as two Mk 46s. Even more potent are the S-3 Viking ASW airplanes that are launched from carrier decks. These can carry much heavier loads of Mk 46s, depth charges or bombs to points over 1000 nm out from the Group at speeds better than three times that of any helicopter. (In addition, the S-3B version of the Viking, joining the fleet in 1987, can launch an antiship Harpoon missile.) If this otherwise impressive ASW weapons system has a weakness, it lies in the too small and too slow Mk 46 torpedo, which is nearly 25 years old and needs a more capable replacement.

There is one final class of antisubmarine weapons that deserves mention: mines. Mines can, in fact, be quite dangerous to submarines because they are small and noiseless and are therefore difficult for the submarine's sensors to locate. One of the most interesting ASW mines at present is the CAPTOR, a weapon that is moored in deep water, where it can acoustically detect passing submarines. It ignores all passing surface ships and may even be set to ignore the first few hostile submarines that pass, but when it is ready to go into action it launches a Mk 46 homing torpedo at its target. Other mines, such as the Quickstrike and the SLMM, are shallow-water weapons that threaten both submarines and surface ships. By the mid-1980s no US surface ships carried mines as offensive weapons, the task of mine-laying being confined solely to submarines and airplanes.

Because submarines can attack surface ships from great distances with missiles, part of the threat they pose is aerial, and to that extent involves the same antiair weaponry that ships use against enemy aircraft. Probably the Navy's most elaborate total AA system is that embarked in a Battle Group, since the carrier's air wing is one of the system's major components. A Battle Group's air defenses are considered to consist of three zones. The outer zone, approximately 90-200 nm from the Group's center, is primarily the province of the defending aircraft of the Group's combat air patrol, or CAP. The CAP is composed mainly of F-14 Tomcat fighters, often assisted by F/A-18 Hornet fighterbombers. In times of threat it may also include E-2C Hawkeye airborne early warning aircraft, which can both extend the Group's radar horizon to 400 nm and, during combat, serve as air controllers for the fighters.

The swing-wing Mach 2.3 Tomcat is the oldest of the current generation of American fighters (*ie*, the generation that includes the Air Force's Eagle and Falcon and the Navy's Hornet), but many analysts still consider it the most capable of all, probably the most sophisticated and deadly fighter ever made. One of the several reasons why it is so formidable is that it is the only aircraft able to launch the Phoenix, the world's longest-range air-to-air missile. Tomcats are able to fire off six Phoenixes simultaneously, all under individual control, at separate airborne targets up to 110 nm away. A new version of the Tomcat, the F-14D, with greatly improved

avionics and 39 percent more thrust will join the fleet in the late 1980s, making this already awesome fighter even more daunting.

The Hornet, though somewhat slower and more lightly armed than the Tomcat and capable of controlling only one missile at a time, is nevertheless an able interceptor. At present it carries Sparrow and Sidewinder air-to-air missiles, and when the Sparrow's replacement, the new fire-and-forget AMRAAM missile, with its 50-nm range, enters service in the late 1980s, the Hornet's potency will be considerably enhanced.

Any enemy aircraft or missiles that penetrate the fighters' outer defensive zone must next pass through the intermediate zone, which extends approximately 10-90 nm from the Group's center. This is the arena in which the ships' larger surface-to-air missiles come into play. As of the second half of the 1980s the Navy's best SAM was the Standard SM-2MR, with a range of up to 90 nm and the larger, two-stage Standard SM-2ER, with a range of 90+ nm and capable of being fitted with a small nuclear warhead. Under consideration is a SM-3, so far officially described only as being 'very long-range.'

ABOVE: *A Standard SM-2ER anti-aircraft missile closes in on a target drone.*
LEFT: *The swing-wing F-14 Tomcat is considered by many to be the world's most formidable fighter.*

RIGHT: *A 3000-round-per-minute Mk 15 Phalanx CIWS (Close-in Weapons System) 20-mm AA gun in action.*
BELOW: *CV 67* John F Kennedy *launches a high-speed Sea Sparrow antiaircraft missile.*

Of course any AA weapon, whatever else its attributes, is only useful if it can hit incoming aerial targets, no meagre challenge if the target is a small, fast enemy missile protected by an aura of electronic countermeasures. Both versions of the Navy's Standard AA missiles carry semi-active homing devices, so that if they can be brought into close enough proximity to an approaching target they have a good chance of destroying it. The problem is to achieve that proximity through constant mid-course corrections of the missiles' flight paths. In other words, the AA missiles' effectiveness is heavily dependent on the quality of the ship-borne radar fire-control systems that guide them.

The most advanced such system in the Navy – and in the world – is one that began to be installed on *Ticonderoga* class cruisers in the mid-1980s. Called 'Aegis,' it is centered on an extraordinary new fixed-array air-search/fire-control radar, the SPY-1, and three clusters of four big computers that digest the information coming from the radar antennas and other sensors, that evaluate and designate priority targets and that then automatically select, launch and control the AA missiles – SM-2MRs. One Aegis system can engage about 20 targets simultaneously, at any altitude (including sea level) and under the most adverse electronic countermeasures conditions. A slightly less capable variant of Aegis is also due to be installed on carriers and on the new *Arleigh Burke* class destroyers that will begin to enter the fleet by the end of the 1980s.

Aegis is only the newest and best of the fire-control systems that, in one form or another, are carried by all major escort ships. How well any of these systems would be able to stand up to heavy air attacks is still a subject of some debate, but, theoretically at least, almost any intermediate-range defensive system could be overwhelmed by sheer saturation. This is why the Group's inner defensive zone remains important.

At present, the Navy's inner AA defenses rely mainly on two short-range weapons: the Sea Sparrow missile and the 20-mm six-barrel Phalanx 'gatling' gun. The Sea Sparrow is an exceptionally fast missile with a 10-nm range. But since it homes in on radar reflections continuously bouncing off an incoming target, it requires a dedicated ship-borne fire-control illuminator throughout its flight – a real limitation for small ships with only one missile director. Thus by the mid-1980s the Navy was actively looking for a replacement for the Sea Sparrow. The leading candidate was a small missile called the RAM that does not require continuous target illumination, but there was also some interest in developing a ship-to-air version of the AMRAAM air-to-air missile now being produced for Navy and Air Force fighter planes. The advantage of the AMRAAM is that it carries a more capable passive radar/infrared guidance system; its disadvantage is its greater size and higher cost.

The Phalanx may be the fastest-firing AA gun in the world, capable of expending a full 989-round magazine of 20-mm depleted-uranium-core projectiles in just under 20 seconds. It has a range of over 1600 yards, and each gun contains in its housing two radars, one to follow the target's path and one to follow the path of the projectile stream, and a computer that automatically aims the gun so that the two paths intersect. By the end of the 1980s over 250 Navy ships will mount from one to four of the current Phalanx units, and already the Navy is developing similar weapons with improved fire-control and larger magazines containing 25-mm or 30-mm projectiles.

Taken as a whole, the Navy's antiaircraft defenses are impressive, but whether they could resist every possible level of saturation attack is unknown. Also, it should be borne in mind that the ideal three-zone AA defense just described applies only to carrier-centered Battle Groups. Battleship-centered Surface Action Groups and other task forces lacking fighter protection would be obliged to rely on the defenses they could mount only in the intermediate and close-in zones. This is the principal reason why many in the Navy continue to argue for the construction of a class of small carriers, 'austere' in design but nevertheless capable of embarking Tomcats or Hornets, that could escort surface forces other than Battle Groups. So far this argument has been stoutly resisted by big-carrier advocates, who fear that such a program might both divert scarce funds from new big-carrier construction and dissipate naval air strength. But if there were no such things as budget restraints the small carriers would obviously make very desirable additions to the fleet.

The principal offensive sea-control weapons carried by US surface ships – Tomahawk and Harpoon cruise missiles – have already been mentioned. Apart perhaps from the

LEFT: *The Mk 45 is the Navy's standard 5-in gun mount. A laser-guided projectile, similar to the Army's Copperhead, is being developed for it.*
BELOW: *A target ship after being hit by a Harpoon missile.*

16-inch guns carried by battleships, conventional naval ordnance plays a decidedly secondary role in the current offensive weapons suite. Many cruisers, destroyers and amphibious assault ships still mount dual-purpose 5-in/54-cal guns for sea fighting and shore bombardment, and by the 1990s these may be capable of firing laser-guided projectiles up to ranges of about 26,000 yards. But all smaller-caliber guns are considered to be primarily AA weapons, just as the ubiquitous surface-launched Mk 46 torpedoes are considered ASW weapons.

Power projection and sea control may be defined as the Navy's classic missions, but in a sense they are both only means to the broader end of winning wars on land. In recognition of this, since the early 1980s Secretary of the Navy John F Lehman, Jr, had been insisting that strategic sealift - the ability of the Navy to ferry large bodies of US troops and matériel to foreign battlefields – must be considered the Navy's third primary mission. Against a background of a deeply eroded US merchant marine and merchant ship-building capacity, the Navy has, since 1982, spent more money on sealift than it had spent in all the previous years since the end of World War II. By 1991 it is estimated that sealift capacity will have grown 700 percent over what it was in 1980, but, given the magnitude of the requirement, this may still be only a fraction of what might be needed.

Planners now see combined air/sealift requirements as falling into two phases-each for the three most likely theaters of conflict: Europe, the Indian Ocean littoral and Northeast Asia. In each area the two phases would be the initial, or 'surge,' lift needed to support the first three to four weeks of fighting and the much larger sustaining lift needed thereafter. For example, the surge requirement for Europe envisages delivery of six Army divisions, 60 Air Force tactical squadrons and one Marine Amphibious Brigade in a matter of 10 days. The subsequent sustaining lift should have the capacity to deliver the equivalent of 10 Army divisions, 88 tactical squadrons and a Marine brigade within a month, and again in each successive 30-day period thereafter, as well as being able to provide continuous resupply to all forces already in the field.

Thanks to the Rapid Deployment Strategy, with its Maritime Prepositioning Forces and designated air transport squadrons already in being, America's capacity to meet surge phase requirements is fairly well in hand. But the sustaining phase is another matter. Airlift, a secondary element in the surge phase, would be almost insignificant in the sustaining phase. Up to 95 percent of all drygoods and 99 percent of all fuel would have to be delivered by sea, and the total requirement for Europe alone would be around 1.5 million tons every 30 days. Where will the Navy find the ships for requirements of such magnitude? (Just to transport a single Army division about 10 specialized, or 30-40 unspecialized, cargo ships are needed.)

A few fleet auxiliary vessels might be pressed into service, but they are really more needed to sustain the fleet itself. There are about 35 ships in the Military Sealift Command that could serve as cargo carriers, and there are about 85 ships in the Ready Reserve section of the mothball fleet (the so-called National Defense Reserve Force) that might be got to sea within 20 days. (The remaining 80 would need about 60 days.) Beyond that there are whatever ships might be recquisitioned from the much-diminished fleet of approximately 250 merchant vessels that fly the American flag throughout the world.

The Navy is slowly trying to enlarge both the core of useful ships in the Military Sealift Command and in the Ready Reserve section of the NDRF. (It hopes to have a total of 116 Ready Reserve ships by 1991.) But little can be done about the decayed US merchant marine, which now carries only about six percent of all America's seaborne commerce. Fortunately, with respect to Europe, NATO maintains a pool of some 600 merchant ships that could be pressed into service in a more-or-less timely fashion, but apart from some commitments from South Korea no similar foreign assets exist in other parts of the world. The most optimistic estimate for non-European theaters is that US sealift might be able to meet up to 85 percent of what is required, but this estimate does *not* take into account wartime attrition, which is bound to be very high. So the problems besetting this third mission of the US Navy are serious, and how they are to be solved is far from clear.

The navy oiler AO 98
Caloosahatchee *of the* Ashtabula *class.*

Organization and Inventory

The way the Navy – and, indeed, the whole US Military – is organized is simply a logical response to its perceived missions and the way they fit into the overall warmaking requirements of the nation. At the working level the US military establishment is divided into nine major commands. Three of these are called Specified Commands, and all three – Aerospace Defense, Strategic Air and Military Airlift – are run by the Air Force. The other six, called Unified Commands, involve, in varying degrees, all the services. The six Unified Commands are: The Atlantic Command, the Pacific Command, and European Command, the Central (*ie*, Southwest Asian or Indian Ocean) Command, the Southern (*ie*, Central and Latin American) Command and the Readiness Command (the Army and Air Force Reserve). The commander-in-chief of each Unified Command usually comes from the most important service in it. Thus the commanders of the Atlantic and Pacific Commands are usually admirals, whereas the commander of the European Command is usually an Air Force or Army general.

The major naval components of these Unified Commands are the Fleets. There are four Fleets: the Second, Third, Sixth and Seventh. The Second Fleet is the primary component of the Atlantic Command. It normally includes about five carriers, some 60 surface combatants, up to 40 attack submarines, about 25 amphibious vessels, a Maritime Prepositioning Squadron and so on, as well as one Marine division and its air wing. It is, in a sense, supplemented by the smaller Sixth Fleet, which nevertheless operates in the Mediterranean and thus falls under the European Command. The Sixth usually includes at least two carriers, about 15 surface combatants, perhaps fours SSNs and five amphibious ships, plus a Marine Amphibious Unit. The other two Fleets operate in the Pacific, the Third in the Eastern Pacific and the smaller Seventh in the Western Pacific. Together they would normally dispose of about six carriers, around 80 surface combatants, perhaps 35 SSNs and a similar number of amphibious ships and a couple of Marine divisions. The precise composition of these fleets of course varies over time and in accordance with specific needs as they arise.

Within the fleets are various tactical units such as Battle Groups, Surface Action Groups, Amphibious Squadrons and the like, also variously composed. A typical small Battle Group might consist of a carrier, at least one Aegis cruiser, a couple of guided missile destroyers and two or three ASW destroyers or frigates. A typical small Amphibious Squadron might include an amphibious assault ship, an amphibious transport/dock, some LSTs and a couple of frigate escorts. Any such units may, as the need arises, either be transferred to another Fleet or Command, or be sent temporarily into waters outside their normal operating areas, as were the Sixth and Seventh Fleet Battle Groups and Amphibious Squadrons that have periodically been deployed in the Indian Ocean.

The approximately 200,000 men and women of the Marine Corps are formed into three Marine Amphibious Forces (MAFs), each consisting of one Marine division, its air wing and its support group. An MAF comprises over 48,000 Marines and about 2400 Navy personnel and would be allo-

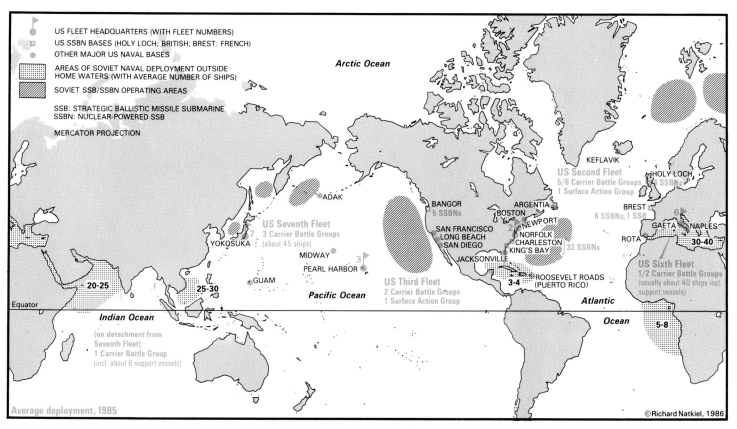

US FLEET HEADQUARTERS (WITH FLEET NUMBERS)
US SSBN BASES (HOLY LOCH: BRITISH; BREST: FRENCH)
OTHER MAJOR US NAVAL BASES
AREAS OF SOVIET NAVAL DEPLOYMENT OUTSIDE
HOME WATERS (WITH AVERAGE NUMBER OF SHIPS)
SOVIET SSB/SSBN OPERATING AREAS
SSB: STRATEGIC BALLISTIC MISSILE SUBMARINE
SSBN: NUCLEAR-POWERED SSB
MERCATOR PROJECTION

Arctic Ocean

KEFLAVIK
US Second Fleet
5/6 Carrier Battle Groups
1 Surface Action Group
HOLY LOCH
SSBNs

BANGOR
5 SSBNs
ARGENTIA
BOSTON
BREST
6 SSBNs, 1 SSB

ADAK

US Seventh Fleet
3 Carrier Battle Groups
(about 45 ships)

YOKOSUKA

NEWPORT
SAN FRANCISCO
LONG BEACH
SAN DIEGO
NORFOLK
CHARLESTON
KING'S BAY
32 SSBNs

GAETA NAPLES
ROTA
30-40

MIDWAY
JACKSONVILLE

PEARL HARBOR

US Sixth Fleet
1/2 Carrier Battle Groups
(usually about 40 ships incl.
support vessels)

3

GUAM

US Third Fleet
2 Carrier Battle Groups
1 Surface Action Group

ROOSEVELT ROADS
(PUERTO RICO)
3-4

Pacific Ocean

20-25

25-30

Equator

Indian Ocean

Atlantic

Ocean

5-8

(on detachment from
Seventh Fleet):
1 Carrier Battle Group
(incl. about 6 support vessels)

Average deployment, 1985

©Richard Natkiel, 1986

LEFT: *The disposition and average strengths of the US Fleets in the mid-1980s. Shown also are the Soviet Navy's operating areas.*

cated about 50 ships for transport. Sub-units of MAFs are the 15,000-man Marine Amphibious Brigade (made up of a Regimental Landing Team and its composite air group) and the 2350-man Marine Amphibious Unit (made up of a Battalion Landing Team and its composite air squadron). In all, the Marine Corps has about 400 fighter and attack aircraft, 600 assault and utility helicopters, over 1000 tanks and landing vehicles.

As of early 1987 the Navy, including the Marine Corps, was composed of about 569,000 men and women. In its inventory it had 562 ships, broken down as follows:

Nuclear Ballistic Missile Submarines 37
Aircraft carriers (deployable) 14
Battleships 3
Nuclear attack submarines 99
Diesel attack submarines 4
Cruisers 35
Destroyers 69
Frigates 114
Patrol combatants 6
Amphibious ships 62
Mine countermeasure ships 3
Underway replenishment ships 57
Strategic support ships 6
Support Forces ships 53

By 1987 the combined Navy and Marine air force operated approximately 6300 aircraft (after the USAAF, the Soviet Air Force and the Chinese Air Force, the largest air force in the world). Of this total about 2000 were accounted as combat airplanes with an additional force of some 300 combat helicopters.

The Navy had originally proposed to build new ships at an average rate of 21.5 per year between 1987 and 1991, but when the Defense Budget for FY 1988 was announced the Administration's request for new ship construction in that year was reduced 33 percent, from 24 to 16. In profile the 1988 military budget seemed to indicate both growing concern about the national deficit and a heightened emphasis on ICBM and SLBM launch capabilities, as well as on new hi-tech weapons systems such as those associated with the Strategic Defense Initiative and stealth aircraft. Procurement of conventional weapons, including several types of ships (though not submarines), suffered accordingly.

Does this mean that the Navy's goal of a 600-ship fleet by the end of 1990 could be in jeopardy? Probably not, for even at a countinuing rate of only 16 new ships a year the Navy would still have a theoretical total of 610 ships in 1990 and 626 in 1991. But these notional figures do not take into account the inevitable retirement of older ships, sometimes in whole blocks. Such retirements may be delayed or strung out, but they cannot be indefinitely postponed. Thus the critical period for the Navy's inventory of deployable fighting ships may come not at the beginning of the decade of the 1990s, but towards its end.

LEFT: *Admiral James D Watkins was CNO during much of Lehman's tenure as Navy Secretary.*
RIGHT: *CVN 69* Dwight D Eisenhower *refueling at sea. Most carriers remain on station considerably longer than the six months that is supposed to be normal.*

The Opposition

That today's US Navy is extremely powerful is hardly in question, but that power is meaningful only in relation to the strength of its great potential rival, the Soviet Navy. Although detailed analysis of Soviet naval power lies beyond the scope of this book, at least a few remarks on the subject are possible. The Soviet Navy is a very large, modern and capable force. It possesses nearly three times as many ships as the US Navy, yet the US Navy has a greater aggregate tonnage. This implies that the Soviet Navy must have a different composition, and the following summary of Soviet warship categories (as of 1986) will suggest in what ways:

Ballistic missile submarines (nuclear) 63
Ballistic missile submarines (diesel) 15
Aircraft carriers ....0 (2 building)
V/STOL carriers 4
Battleships 0
Battle cruisers (nuclear) 2
Cruise missile submarines (nuclear) 65
Attack submarines (nuclear) 72
Attack submarines (diesel) 147
Cruisers 37
Destroyers 66
Frigates 197
Corvettes 148
Amphibious warfare ships 73
Other ....*c* 700
Naval air force ....1635 (aircraft/helo)

Perhaps the most obvious difference in the composition of the two fleets lies in the contrast between their emphases on carriers and submarines. At present the Soviets have no true carriers at all, though two 65,000-tonners are under construction. The US expects to have 15 large carriers by the early 1990s, and as of December 1986 the Defense Department had requested authorization for two additional *Nimitz* class nuclear carriers to join the fleet in the second half of the '90s. On the other hand, the Soviets deploy nearly twice as many SSBNs as the US and a significantly larger number of SSNs (cruise missile and/or attack). In addition, the Soviets

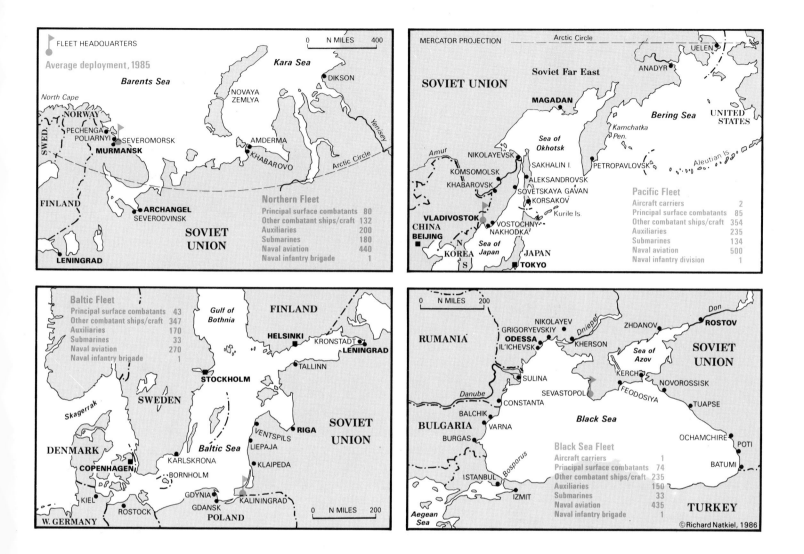

FLEET HEADQUARTERS

Average deployment, 1985

Barents Sea
Kara Sea
DIKSON
North Cape
NOVAYA ZEMLYA
NORWAY
SWED.
PECHENGA
POLIARNYI
SEVEROMORSK
AMDERMA
MURMANSK
KHABAROVO
Arctic Circle
Yenisey
FINLAND
ARCHANGEL
SEVERODVINSK
SOVIET UNION
LENINGRAD

Northern Fleet
Principal surface combatants	80
Other combatant ships/craft	132
Auxiliaries	200
Submarines	180
Naval aviation	440
Naval infantry brigade	1

MERCATOR PROJECTION
Arctic Circle
UELEN
Soviet Far East
ANADYR
SOVIET UNION
MAGADAN
Bering Sea
UNITED STATES
Sea of Okhotsk
Kamchatka Pen.
Amur
NIKOLAYEVSK
SAKHALIN I.
PETROPAVLOVSK
Aleutian Is.
KOMSOMOLSK
KHABAROVSK
ALEKSANDROVSK
SOVETSKAYA GAVAN
KORSAKOV
Kurile Is.
VLADIVOSTOK
CHINA
BEIJING
VOSTOCHNY
NAKHODKA
KOREA
N
S
Sea of Japan
JAPAN
TOKYO

Pacific Fleet
Aircraft carriers	2
Principal surface combatants	85
Other combatant ships/craft	354
Auxiliaries	235
Submarines	134
Naval aviation	500
Naval infantry division	1

Baltic Fleet
Principal surface combatants	43
Other combatant ships/craft	347
Auxiliaries	170
Submarines	33
Naval aviation	270
Naval infantry brigade	1

Gulf of Bothnia
FINLAND
HELSINKI
KRONSTADT
LENINGRAD
TALLINN
STOCKHOLM
RIGA
SWEDEN
SOVIET UNION
Skagerrak
VENTSPILS
LIEPAJA
DENMARK
Baltic Sea
KARLSKRONA
KLAIPEDA
COPENHAGEN
BORNHOLM
KIEL
GDYNIA
KALININGRAD
ROSTOCK
GDANSK
W. GERMANY
POLAND

Don
NIKOLAYEV
ZHDANOV
ROSTOV
GRIGORYEVSKIY
Dnieper
RUMANIA
ODESSA
IL'ICHEVSK
KHERSON
SOVIET UNION
Sea of Azov
KERCH
NOVOROSSISK
SULINA
SEVASTOPOL
FEODOSIYA
TUAPSE
Danube
CONSTANTA
BALCHIK
Black Sea
BULGARIA
VARNA
OCHAMCHIRE
POTI
BURGAS
Black Sea Fleet
BATUMI
ISTANBUL
IZMIT
TURKEY
Aegean Sea
Bosporus

Black Sea Fleet
Aircraft carriers	1
Principal surface combatants	74
Other combatant ships/craft	235
Auxiliaries	150
Submarines	33
Naval aviation	435
Naval infantry brigade	1

©Richard Natkiel, 1986

LEFT TOP: *The helicopter cruiser* Moskva.

LEFT: *Soviet amphibious forces include two ships of the* Ivan Rogov *class, each able to carry four helos and three 85-ton air-cushion landing craft.*

ABOVE: *The disposition and average strengths of the Soviet Fleets in the mid-1980s.*

have a very large number of diesel submarines, a warship category the US has all but abandoned.

US emphasis on big carriers results in an American naval airforce that is nearly four times as large as its Soviet counterpart, and American Tomcats and Hornets are vastly more capable than the Yak-38 Forger fighters now deployed on the 36,000-ton Soviet V/STOL carriers. But Soviet land-based long-range naval bombers – notably the famous supersonic Tu-26 Backfire, with its stand-off air-to-surface missiles, and its larger, more advanced successor, the Blackjack – could pose a major threat even in the absence of Soviet carriers.

In one important respect, a category-by-category comparison of the US and Soviet fleets may be misleading, for Soviet naval planners have to take into account not just the US Navy but the fleets of America's NATO allies as well. For example, NATO (including France) would add to the American totals 10 more SSBNs, 139 attack submarines (18 nuclear), nine small carriers, 93 destroyers, 138 frigates, 120 corvettes and so on. As a result, the US has deliberately chosen to curtail new construction in certain ship categories in which other NATO navies are already strong.

As to weaponry, it is difficult to make comparisons between the US and Soviet Navies. Only in the category of naval mines does one side – the Soviet – seem to have a clear advantage. In general, the Soviet Navy seems to lead in volume of firepower, while the US Navy seems to lead in fire-control and missile guidance, various types of sophisticated sensors and the like. What these differences might mean in terms of success in battle is imponderable, and in any case, they are all very much subject to change over time.

In sum, the Soviet Navy, though in many ways different in concept and structure from the US Navy, has the material capability of being a very serious opponent. How the two navies would be employed strategically in case of war would therefore have an important bearing on which would best succeed in gaining victory.

Strategies

Both US and Soviet naval strategies, driven by new technologies, have been – and are still – constantly changing. In the late 1970s US strategy was still focused on controlling various 'choke points', gaps such as those between the United Kingdom and Iceland, Iceland and Greenland or Japan and Kamchatka, through which Soviet submarines and ships would have to pass to gain access to the open seas. But by the early 1980s both the lengthening range of Soviet ballistic and cruise missiles and the growing capabilities of Soviet attack submarines made this choke-point strategy seem increasingly inadequate. Now Soviet SSBNs could stay close to homewater 'bastions' in the Kara/Barents Sea area off Northern Europe and in the Sea of Okhostk off Eastern Siberia and still threaten the continental US. By the same token, Soviet SSNs seemed to have a steadily improving chance of slipping through the choke points and menacing Allied ships – especially sealift ships and carriers – on the oceans.

Accordingly, in the mid-1980s US and NATO naval policy shifted to a more aggressive strategy of 'forward defense,' whereby in the event of war the Soviet bastions would immediately become priority targets for concentrated naval and air attack. Since the bastions are powerfully defended by Soviet SSNs, surface ships, land-based aircraft and mines, attacks on them by Allied SSNs and land- and carrier-based aircraft would inevitably be very costly. Some critics of this

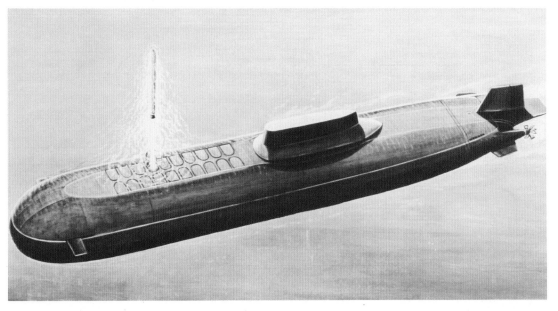

ABOVE: *The world's largest SSBNs, the Soviet* Typhoon *boats appear to be designed to operate under the Arctic ice pack.*

forward policy have argued (a) that it probably cannot succeed, (b) that it would squander Allied SSNs, leaving too few available to hunt down their ship-threatening Soviet counterparts on the open seas and (c) that if the strategy by chance did seem to be succeeding, the Soviets, rather than permit an important part of their strategic nuclear triad to be destroyed, would be strongly motivated to escalate to an all-out nuclear exchange.

Whatever the merits of these criticisms, the Soviets themselves seem to have taken the forward strategy seriously enough to begin experimenting with ways of moving their SSBNs outside the confines of the bastions without running unacceptably high risks of detection and destruction. At present the favored area for the possible re-location of the Soviet SSBNs seems to be under the Arctic ice cap, and both navies are now furiously pressing forward to develop the technologies necessary to make submarine and antisubmarine warfare feasible in this forbidding environment. This is surely one reason why the US Navy has given such high priority to the rapid development of the formidable new *Seawolf* class of attack submarines, larger, quieter, deeper-diving successors to the *Los Angeles* SSNs, already the most sophisticated attack submarines deployed by any navy in the world.

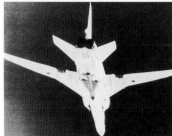

LEFT: *A Department of Defense illustration of a Soviet* Kiev *class V/STOL carrier in a floating dock. The* Kievs *carry a small (c 30) compliment of helos and V/STOL fighters.*
ABOVE: *The Soviet TU-26 Backfire is a sophisticated Mach 2.2 long-range land-based bomber that is a specialist in ship attack.*

Because American SSBNs have never had to cope with choke points, no US equivalent of the bastion strategy ever evolved. American 'boomers' are widely dispersed, ranging over 30 million square miles of open ocean on secret, solitary patrols. With the advent of the 6000-nm-range Trident D-5 submarine-launched ballistic missile in the early 1990s, the area in which American SSBNs can operate will expand to 50 million square miles. Even now, the Navy claims, these boats are essentially undetectable.

The growth of Soviet naval power has had one other basic effect on US naval strategy. In the 1970s, when the US fleet had eroded to a nadir of less than 460 ships, it was necessary – and still possible – to think in terms of a 'swing strategy,' in which some ships of the US Pacific Fleets would be transferred to the Atlantic to help out in times of crisis. But now that the Soviet Pacific Fleet has grown to be a major force (approximately two V/STOL carriers, 200 surface combatants, 90 submarines and so on), no such option remains. Henceforward, the US will never safely be able to maintain less than a fully viable two-ocean navy.

Chapter 2
AIRCRAFT AND WEAPONS OF THE FLEET

A Navy F-4 Phantom fighterbomber circles over CV 41 Midway in the China Sea.

Naval Aircraft

As of 1986 the Navy's air force operated the following numbers of first-line combat squadrons:

Fighter (F-14 Tomcat; F-4 Phantom-II) 24
Fighter/attack (F/A-18 Hornet) 3
Light attack (A-7E Corsair) 22
Heavy attack (A-6E and KA-6D Intruder) 12
Electronic warfare (EA-6B Prowler) 9
Airborne early warning (E-2B/C Hawkeye) 12
Antisubmarine (S-3A Viking) 11
Helicopter antisubmarine (SH-3H Sea King; SH-60B Seahawk) .12
Light helicopter antisubmarine (SH-2F Seasprite) 6
Land-based patrol (P-3B/C Orion) 24

The carrier-borne portion of this force was organized into 13 carrier air wings, with a 14th due to be activated when the *Theodore Roosevelt* became operational. Presumably a 15th will be activated in the early 1990s if the number of big carriers in the fleet rises to 15. In addition to its front-line squadrons, the Navy also maintains 34 additional squadrons in its Naval Reserve Force.

The Marine air force operated three air wings (of considerably different size and composition), plus one in reserve. In all, the Marine air force included 30 squadrons of tactical aircraft (including Harriers, Hornets, Phantoms, Intruders, tankers and Ov-10 Bronco reconnaissance aircraft), 29 squadrons of lift, attack or utility helicopters and eight squadrons devoted to command support or training.

By the early 1990s Hornets and advanced versions of the Tomcat will probably have replaced most or all of the remaining Phantoms and Corsairs. By that time, too, we may have some inkling of what kinds of new aircraft the Navy will be operating after the year 2000. The following is a brief summary of the principal combat aircraft now in service in the Navy and Marine Corps.

ABOVE: *An F-14 Tomcat, its wings extended, being catapulted from the deck of CVN 70 Carl Vinson.* RIGHT: *Two Tomcats, their wings full back and wearing a livery of experimental camouflage.*

Grumman F-14A/D Tomcat

Held by many to be the world's most capable fighter, the all-weather Tomcat is a two-place, variable geometry Mach 2-plus carrier interceptor. It is the only plane capable of launching and controlling (simultaneously) up to six 110-nm-range Phoenix air-to-air missiles. The F-14D, scheduled to begin replacing the F-14A in 1988, will receive 39 percent more thrust from its new GE F-110 engines, plus a much-improved digitalized AWG-9 radar fire-control system and other advanced avionics. (The following specifications relate to the F-14A.)

Power: Two 20,900 lb st (with reheat) P&W TF30-P-414A turbofans

Max speed: Mach 2.34

Combat radius (without air/air refueling): 500+ nm

Dimensions: Span: 64 ft 1½ in/38 ft 2½in; length: 62 ft 8 in

Armament: One 20 mm M61 Vulcan multi-barrel cannon. Various stores, *eg* six Phoenix/two Sidewinder *or* two Phoenix/two Sidewinder/three Sparrow *or* up to 14,500 lb of bombs, including nuclear.

An F/A-18 Hornet of Fighterbomber Squadron 125.

McDonnell Douglas F/A-18A Hornet

Just beginning to enter the fleet, this single-seat dual-purpose carrier aircraft can switch at will between fighter and bomber modes. It is intended to serve both as the fleet's principal light attack bomber and as a back-up fighter for the F-14. Its computerized fire-control system is based on the Hughes APG-65 radar. The Navy and Marines have 1377 Hornets on order.

Power: Two 16,000 lb st (with reheat) GE F404-GE-400 turbofans

Max speed: Mach 1.8

Combat radius (without air/air refueling): 400+ nm

Dimensions: Span: 37 ft 6 in; length 56 ft

Armament: One 20 mm M61 Vulcan multi-barrel cannon. In fighter mode, two Sidewinder/four Sparrow. In bomber mode, up to 17,000 lb of various stores, including nuclear. As on other Navy fighter aircraft, the Sidewinders may eventually be replaced by AMRAAMs.

McDonnell Douglas F-4N/S Phantom

Being phased out of front-line naval service in favor of Tom-cats and Hornets, this world-famous veteran two-seat fighter-bomber was no longer deployed on fleet carriers as of 1987, but it was still well represented in the Marine air force and the Naval Reserve. A reconnaissance version, the RF-4B, is to be fitted with General Electric J79-GE-10B smokeless engines. 235 older F4-B/J will be up-graded to N/S standards.

Power:	Two 17,100 lb st (with reheat) GE J79-GE-8 turbofans
Max speed:	Mach 2.2
Combat radius (without air/air refueling):	900 nm
Dimensions:	Span: 39 ft 7½ in; length: 58 ft 1½ in
Armament:	Four Sparrow/four Sidewinder *or* up to 15,450 lb of various stores, including nuclear.

An F-4J Phantom fighterbomber of Fighter Squadron 92.

McDonnell Douglas A-4M Skyhawk

This elderly, but still capable, single-place attack bomber is no longer a front-line naval combat plane but is still used by the Marines and the Naval Reserve.

Power: One 11,200 lb st P&W J52-P-408 turbojet

Max speed: Mach .94

Combat radius (without air/air refueling): 150 nm

Dimensions: Span: 27 ft 6 in; length: 40 ft 3 ¾ in

Armament: Two 20-mm Mk 12 cannon. Up to 9155 lb of stores.

Grumman A-6E/F (and KA-6D) Intruder

This is the Navy's standard carrier heavy attack bomber and will remain so well into the 1990s. Throughout its long service life the two-place Intruder has been continuously up-graded. It has most recently been fitted with a new Target Recognition-Attack Multisensor system and is due to receive a synthetic aperture radar and expanded missile launch capabilities. The A-6F, scheduled to join the fleet in 1989, is to be powered by two GE 404 engines. It will have a maximum speed of around Mach .9, a combat radius of 600+ nm, STOL capability, improved avionics and self-defense systems and the ability to launch large missiles such as Harpoon, HARM, Maverick and others. The KA-6D tanker version of the Intruder carries up to 30,000 lb of fuel for air/air refueling. The Intruder is also used by the Marines and the Naval Reserve. (The following specifications relate to the A-6E.)

Power: Two 9300 lb st P&W J52-P-8 turbojets

Max speed: 654 mph

Combat radius (without air/air refueling): 450+ nm

Dimensions: Span: 53 ft; length: 54 ft 9 in

Armament: Up to 18,000 lb of various stores, including nuclear. Most A-6Es are now capable of launching Sidewinder, Harpoon, Maverick, Walleye, Bullpup etc missiles.

ABOVE: *An A-4M Skyhawk.*
LEFT: *The KA-6 tanker version of the Intruder.*

RIGHT: *These A-6 Intruder attack bombers belong to the Air Wing of CV 61 Ranger.*

ABOVE: *An A-7 Corsair II attack bomber of Attack Squadron 82.*
ABOVE RIGHT: *An AV-8A Harrier V/STOL fighter of Marine Fighter Squadron 513, the first US unit to receive the plane.*
LEFT: *An S-3A Viking ASW plane on the deck of CV 63 Kitty hawk.*

Ling-Temco-Vought A-7E Corsair II

This 20-year-old single-seat carrier light attack bomber will probably be phased out of front-line service in favor of the Hornet by the end of the 1980s. Some consideration is, however, being given to a radical up-date of the aircraft that would make it into an all-weather supersonic (perhaps Mach 1.6) strike fighter. Meantime, existing A-7s are being steadily up-graded by such additions as FLIR sensor pods, ALR-45 radar warning systems, etc.

Power:	One 15,000 lb st Allison TF41-A-2 turbojet
Max speed:	663 mph
Combat radius (without air/air refueling):	425 nm
Dimensions:	Span: 38 ft 8½ in; length 46 ft 1½ in
Armament:	One 20-mm M61 Vulcan multi-barrel cannon/various stores, including nuclear, up to 15,000 lb.

McDonnell Douglas AV-8B Harrier II

This American derivative of the famous single-seat British Aerospace V/STOL fighterbomber is planned to equip 20 Marine attack squadrons by the 1990s. It can operate from the land or from the flight decks of such amphibious assault ships as those of the *Wasp*, *Tarawa* and *Iwo Jima* classes. Because it can vector thrust while in flight its maneuverability is exceptional. Its relatively unsophisticated avionics, however, need up-grading.

Power:	One 21,500 lb st Rolls-Royce F-402-PR-406 vectored-thrust turbofan
Max speed:	Mach .91
Combat radius (without air/air refueling):	VTOL–100+ nm; STOL–300 nm
Dimensions:	Span: 30 ft 4 in; length: 46 ft 4 in
Armament:	Two pod-mounted 30-mm cannon/up to 9200 lb of stores (Sidewinder, Maverick, bombs, etc).

Lockheed S-3A/B (and KS-3A) Viking

This exceptionally sophisticated four-place aircraft is the Navy's principal ASW carrier plane. Ten are assigned to most carrier air wings. It is fitted with a Univac AYK-10 digital computer to process information from its various sensors, which include radar, sonobuoys and a magnetic anomaly detector. The S-3B, which began to join the fleet in 1987, has, in addition, a new synthetic aperture radar, an ECM dispenser and an auxiliary power unit, as well as a Harpoon launch capability. The tanker version of the Viking is known as the KS-3A. (The following specifications relate to the S-3A).

Power:	Two 9275 lb st GE TF-GE-400 turbofans
Max speed:	518 mph
Combat radius:	1150 nm
Dimensions:	Span: 68 ft 8 in; length: 53 ft 4 in
Armament:	60 sonobuoys/four Mk 46 torpedoes/four bombs/four depth charges or mines.

Grumman E-2C Hawkeye

The five-place Hawkeye is the Navy's premier airborne early warning/air-control carrier aircraft. Its big APS-125 radar, carried in a dish-shaped rotating radome atop the fusilage, has a 250-nm range, can track over 600 air and surface targets and can control up to 25 intercepts simultaneously. It is due to receive both improved radar and engines in the late 1980s. Each carrier air wing normally includes four Hawkeyes.

Power:	Two 4910 shp Allison T56-A-425 turboprops
Max speed:	374 mph
Combat radius:	Average loiter @ 200 nm is four hours
Dimensions:	Span: 80 ft 7 in; length; 57 ft 7 in
Armament:	None

Boeing-Bell MV-22 Osprey

Full details of this new tilt-rotor aircraft – due to begin flight testing in the second half of 1987 – were still unavailable as of this writing. Its two engine nacelles can rotate through 90 degrees in the vertical plane, thus permitting the craft to operate either as a helicopter or as a fixed-wing airplane. It is seen primarily as a fast ship-to-shore troop transport for amphibious operations, and the Marines plan to acquire over 550 units when the Osprey enters service in 1991. So far, the Navy's order is confined to 50 units configured for search-and-rescue operations. (The following specifications are provisional.)

Power:	Two 6150 shp Allison T406-AD-400 turboshafts
Max speed:	c 400 mph
Combat radius (fully loaded):	200 nm
Dimensions:	Span: 46 ft 6 in; length: 57 ft 4 in
Capacity:	24 fully equipped troops or 4000 lb of internal cargo, plus up to 10,000 lb of external load.

Grumman EA-6B Prowler

The four-place Prowler, a much-modified version of the Intruder, is a carrier-borne electronic warfare aircraft. It carries an APS-130 radar, five ALQ-99F electronic counter-measure jammer rods beneath the wings and a streamlined electronic-equipment pod atop the vertical stablizer. Four Prowlers are normally assigned to a carrier air wing. A version of the aircraft is also operated by the Marines.

Power:	Two 11,200 lb st P&W J52-P-408 turbojets
Max speed:	613 mph
Combat radius:	710 nm
Dimensions:	Span: 53 ft; length: 59 ft 10 in
Armament:	None

LEFT ABOVE: *An E-2A Hawkeye airborne early warning/air control carrier aircraft.*
LEFT BELOW: *The EA-6B Prowler, ECM version of the Intruder.*

LEFT: *An artist's impression of the new MV-22 Osprey tilt-rotor aircraft due to enter service around 1991.*
BELOW: *A P-3C Orion ASW patrol plane of Patrol Squadron 56.*

Lockheed P-3C Orion

The ten-place (five crew and five tactical team) is the Navy's standard land-based patrol/ASW aircraft. It carries an ASQ-114 computer to analyze data from its APS-115 radar, infrared sensors, magnetic anomaly detectors and other equipment. As of the mid-1980s 233 P-3Cs were in service (plus 281 P-3As and Bs).

Power:	Four 4910 shp Allison T56-A-14 turboprops
Max speed:	473 mph
Combat radius:	2380 nm
Dimension:	Span: 99 ft 8 in; length: 116 ft 10 in
Armament:	Four Mk 46 torpedoes/six mines/two nuclear depth charges/four Harpoon/87 sonobuoys/etc.
	Max internal load: 7252 lb; max underwing load: 12,000 lb.

ABOVE: *A tanker-configured C-130 Hercules refuels a CH-53 Sea Stallion helicopter.*

Other Fixed-Wing Aircraft

The Navy and Marine Corps operate many other types of aircraft. Two additional combat types that can operate from carriers include the twin-engine McDonnell Douglas EA-3B Skywarrior electronics warfare aircraft and the single-place Ling-Temco-Vought RF-8G Crusader photo-reconnaissance plane, a variant of the standard carrier fighter of the early 1960s. Only a handful of these elderly veterans remain in service, and both types could usefully be replaced. Two non-combat carrier types are the Grumman C-1A Trader and C-2A Greyhound, both carrier onboard delivery (COD) types.

Among the land-based types are:

Electronic warfare
EC-130Q Hercules
E-6A (military version of Boeing 707, due to replace EC-130Q in the 1990s)

Observation/air-control/attack
OV-10 Bronco (Marine Corps)
Cargo/Transport
C-4 Academe
C-9 Skytrain
VC-10 Gulfstream
C-12 Huron
CT-29 Sabreliner
C-118 Liftmaster
C-130 Hercules
C-131 Samaritan
Trainers
T-2 Buckeye
T-28 Trojan
T-34 Mentor
T-39 Sabreliner
T-44 King Air
T-46 Hawk

PREVIOUS PAGE: *The SH-3 Sea King is the standard ASW helicopter on carriers and some* Spruance *class destroyers.*

ABOVE: *An SH-2F Seasprite LAMPS-I ASW helicopter with 100-gallon auxiliary gas tanks.*

Sikorsky SH-3D/G/H Sea King

This four-man ASW helicopter was standard equipment on carriers and some destroyers in the mid 1980s. Deliveries of the SH-3H began in 1986, and retrofittings of SH-3Gs to H standards was also begun. (The following specifications relate to the SH-3H.)

Power:	Two 1400 shp GE T58-GE-10 turboshafts
Mission radius:	625 nm
Equipment:	APS-24 radar, ASQ-13 dipping sonar, ASQ-81(V)2 magnetic anomaly detector
Armament:	Two Mk 46 torpedoes

Kaman SH-2F Seasprite LAMPS-I

The three-man Seasprite carried by many cruisers, destroyers and frigates was the first AW helicopter to be fitted out to meet the requirements of the Navy's Light Airborne Multi-Purpose System (LAMPS). Since some older ships cannot accommodate the new Seahawk LAMPS-III, the Seasprite's more capable successor, Seasprites are expected to continue in service through the 1990s.

Power:	Two 1350 shp GE T58-GE-8F turboshafts
Mission radius:	445 nm
Equipment:	LN-66 radar/15 sonobuoys/eight smoke markers/ASQ-81(V)2 magnetic anomaly detector
Armament:	Two Mk 46 torpedoes

Sikorsky SH-60 B/F Seahawk LAMPS-III

By the 1990s the highly sophisticated four-place Seahawk ASW helicopter is intended to replace the Seasprite on all *Ticonderoga* class cruisers, four *Kidd* and 31 *Spruance* class destroyers and 51 *Oliver Hazard Perry* class frigates. The SH-60F, which began entering the fleet in 1986, differs from the earlier model primarily in that it is equipped with an ASQ-13F dipping sonar on a 1500-ft cable. (The following specifications relate to the SH-60B.)

Power:	Two 1723 shp GE T700-GE-401 turbojets
Mission radius:	150 nm
Equipment:	APS-124 radar/25 sonobuoys/ASQ-81(V)2 magnetic anomaly detector/ALQ-142 radar warner/jammer etc. All sensor data is also displayed on the ship controlling the Seahawk.
Armament:	Two Mk 46 torpedoes

ABOVE: *A SH-60 Seahawk LAMPS-III ASW helicopter armed with two Mk 46 torpedoes.*

Boeing Vertol CH-46 (and HH-46) A/D/E Sea Knight

The three-place (crew) CH-46 was still the Marine Corps' standard medium-lift troop-carrying helicopter in the mid-1980s. The cargo-carrying HH46, which can carry 3000 lb internally or 10,000 lb in a sling beneath, is used by both the Navy and the Marines. (The following specifications relate to the CH-46E.)

Power: Two 1870 shp GE T58-GE-10 turboshafts

Mission radius: 540 nm

Capacity: eighteen fully equipped troops

Sikorsky CH-53 A/D (and RH-53D) Sea Stallion

The CH-53 is the Marine Corps' standard heavy-lift troop-carrying helicopter. In its cargo-carrying configurations it can carry up to four tons of freight. The Navy operates the RH-53D as a minesweeper. It is armed with two 12.7 mm machine guns and can tow a variety of acoustic and sonar arrays, cable cutters, a hydrofoil sled, etc. (The following specifications relate to the CH-53D.)

Power: Two 2925 shp GE T64-GE-413 turboshafts

Mission radius: 540 nm

Capacity: Thirty-eight fully equipped troops or 24 occupied stretchers

Sirkosky CH-53E Super Stallion (and MH-53E Sea Dragon)

The Super Stallion, the heaviest-lift helicopter in the Navy's and Marines' inventory, began to enter the fleet in significant quantities in the mid-1980s. The CH-53E is used primarily by the Marines as a troop/cargo-carrier. The MH-53 is used primarily as a Navy minesweeper and can handle all the equipment used by the RH-53D, plus an ALQ-166 magnetic mine countermeasures sled. (The following specifications relate to the CH-53E.)

LEFT: *A CH-53 Sea Knight troop-carrying helicopter landing on the deck of CV 63* Kitty Hawk. BELOW: *A CH-53 Sea Stallion.* RIGHT: *A UH-1H utility helicopter.* RIGHT BELOW: *A CH-53E Super Stallion on the deck of BB 61* Iowa. *The CH-53E can carry 53 fully equipped troops.*

Power: Three 4380 shp GE T64-GE-416 turboshafts

Mission radius: 500 nm with 10 tons of external cargo

Capacity: Fifty-six fully equipped troops or up to 16 tons of cargo

Bell UH-1E/N Iroquois

The Iroquois is primarily a Marine assault helicopter, though the Navy also uses it for utility and training.

Power: Two 900 shp P&W PT6-3B turboshafts

Mission radius: 250 nm

Armament/capacity: Two 7.62 mm machine guns and rockets. Can carry up to 16 troops.

Bell AH-1J/T Sea Cobra and AH-1W Super Cobra

The AH-1 is a Marine helicopter intended primarily for ground attack. The latest version, the AH-1W, due to join the fleet in the late 1980s, will have more powerful engines (T-700s) and a greater lift capacity. (The following specifications relate to the AH-1T.)

Power: Two 1970 shp P&W T400-WV-402 turboshafts

Mission radius: 360 nm

Armament: One 20-mm XM-197 Gatling gun and 76 2.75-in rockets *or* two 7.62-mm miniguns and Hellfire, Sidearm or TOW

FUTURE AIRCRAFT DEVELOPMENTS

The Navy and the USAF are studying the possibility of producing a single fighter aircraft that will replace the Navy's F-14 Tomcat and the Air Force's F-15 Eagle in the late 1990s. They are similarly investigating a single attack replacement for the Intruder and the F-111. Meantime, McDonnell Douglas is well advanced in development of a Mach 2 V/STOL fighter/attack aircraft intended to replace the Harrier (and possibly the Hornet) in the late 1990s. Pratt & Whitney and Rolls-Royce have indicated a willingness to collaborate in developing its engine.

Naval Weapons

BALLISTIC NUCLEAR MISSILES

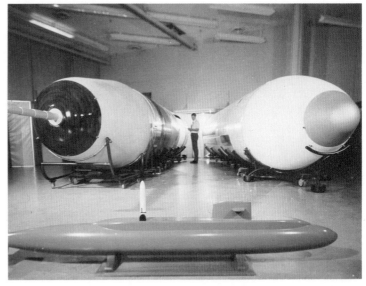

ABOVE: *A Trident-I C-4 ballistic missile fired from beneath the surface by SSBN 727* Michigan. ABOVE RIGHT: *Trident and Poseidon missiles behind a model of an SSBN launching a missile.*

Poseidon (C-3) UGM-73

Length: 34 ft

Propulsion: Two-stage, solid fuel

Guidance: Inertial

Range: 2500 nm (with 14 MIRV) or 3200 nm (with 10 MIRV)

Warhead: Up to 14 independently targetable nuclear warheads (MIRV) of 50 KT

Platform: *Lafayette* class SSBNs

Remarks: Replacement for the Polaris. No longer produced.

Trident I (C-4) UGM-96

Length: 34 ft

Propulsion: Three-stage, solid fuel

Guidance: Inertial

Range: 4350 nm

Warhead: Eight 100 KT MIRV

Platform: *Lafayette* and *Ohio* SSNBs

Remarks: Replacement for the Poseidon. The standard SLBM of the 1980s.

Trident II (D-5)

Length: 44 ft

Propulsion: Three-stage, solid fuel

Guidance: Inertial

Range: 6000 nm

Warhead: 14 MIRV of 150 KT or seven maneuverable warheads (MARV) of 300 KT

Platform: *Ohio* class SSBNs

Remarks: Replacement for the Trident I. To enter service in the late 1980s.

SURFACE-TO-SURFACE MISSILES

Harpoon (RGM-84)

Length: 15ft 2in for surface or submarine launch/12 ft 6 in for air launch

Propulsion: Turbojet (with solid fuel booster)

Guidance: Inertial/active radar homing

Range: 60 nm

Warhead: 510 lbs conventional

Platform: *Permit* and later class SSNs, cruisers, destroyers, frigates, small combatants, several aircraft types

Remarks: An all-weather cruise missile that can be launched from over 280 ships and submarines (submarine version is UGM-84).

Tomahawk (BGM-109)

Versions: Three: strategic (TLAM/N): antiland tactical (TLAM/C): antiship tactical (TASM)

Length: 18 ft 2 in

Propulsion: Turbofan/solid fuel booster

Guidance: Inertial/active radar homing. TLAM/N and TLAM/C also use terrain contour matching (TERCOM) mid-flight. TLAM/C also uses air optical digitalized scene-matching correlator with a 30-ft CEP for homing.

Range: TLAM/N – 1350 nm; TLAM/C – up to 700 nm; TASM – 250 nm

Warhead: TLAM/N – one 200 KT nuclear; TLAM/C and TASM – 972-lb conventional explosive.

Platform: Most SSNs and surface combatants; potentially several aircraft

Remarks: The Navy's newest all-weather cruise missile. It can travel at over 500 mph 50 ft above water.

ABOVE: *A Tomahawk cruise missile at launch time.*

ABOVE LEFT: *A Harpoon antiship missile launched from CG 16 Leahy.*

SURFACE-TO-AIR MISSILES

Sea Sparrow RIM-7

Length:	12 ft
Propulsion:	solid fuel
Guidance:	radar homing
Range:	10 nm
Warhead:	conventional
Platform:	Most surface combatants and many auxiliaries

Remarks: An adaptation of the Sparrow air/air missile used for close-in defense. The current version, RIM-7M, features a monopulse radar. RIM-7 will probably be replaced in the 1990s by either RAM or an adaptation of AMRAAM.

Standard (SM-1MR) RIM-66B

Length:	14 ft 8 in
Propulsion:	Solid fuel, single stage
Guidance:	semiactive radar homing
Range:	20 nm (60,00 ft alt)
Warhead:	Conventional
Platform:	Cruisers, destroyers, frigates

Remarks: The oldest SAM in Navy service. Has been continuously up-graded.

Standard (SM-2MR) RIM-66C

Length: 14 ft

Propulsion: Solid fuel/solid fuel booster

Guidance: Mid-course guidance from surface, plus inertial reference/semiactive radar homing

Range: Up to 90 nm

Warhead: Conventional

Platform: *Ticonderoga* class cruisers

Remarks: Specifically developed for use with Aegis.

Standard (SM-2ER) RIM-67B

Length: 26 ft 2 in

Propulsion: Solid fuel/solid fuel booster

Guidance: Mid-course guidance from surface, plus inertial reference/semi-active radar homing

Range: 90+ nm (80,000 ft alt)

Warhead: Conventional or nuclear

Platform: Cruisers, destroyers, frigates

Remarks: Began to enter the fleet in the early 1980s.

RAM RIM-116A

Length: 9 ft 2 in

Propulsion: Solid fuel

Guidance: Passive radio frequency acquisition and homing, plus infrared homing

Range: *c* 5 nm

Warhead: Conventional

Platform: Potentially many surface types

Remarks: The probable replacement of Sea Sparrow in the 1990s, this is a high-speed (Mach 2+) spin-stablized close-in air defense weapon.

Marine Corps SAM Missiles

The Marines use the Hawk MIM-23B, a 16-ft land-based radar-guided AA missile with a 25-mi range. Also used is the Stinger FIM-92, a small shoulder-launched AA missile..

TOP: *CG 49* Vincennes *launching an ASROC ASW missile.*
ABOVE: *The explosion of an ASROC-launched nuclear depth charge.*
FAR LEFT: *CG 52* Bunker Hill *fires a Standard SM-2MR medium-range AA missile.*
LEFT: *A Sea Sparrow short-range AA missile at launch.*

ANTISUBMARINE MISSILES

ASROC RUR-5A

Length: 15 ft

Propulsion: Solid fuel

Guidance: Ballistic/acoustic homing via Mk 46 torpedo

Range: 6 nm

Warhead: Mk 46 torpedo or nuclear depth bomb

Platform: Cruisers, destroyers, frigates

Remarks: The Navy's standard surface-launched ASW weapon. Drops torpedo by parachute. Aimed by computer linked to sonar.

SUBROC UUM-44A

Length: 21 ft

Propulsion: Solid fuel/solid fuel booster

Guidance: 30 nm

Warhead: Nuclear depth bomb

Platform: Most *Permit* and later class SSNs

Remarks: The Navy's standard submarine-launched ASW missile. Due to be replaced by Sea Lance in the 1990s.

Sea Lance Stand-off-Weapon

Length: *c* 20 ft

Propulsion: Solid fuel

Guidance: Inertial in flight/active-passive acoustic homing (torpedo)

Range: Much greater than SUBROC (some sources estimate 1000+ nm)

Warhead: Nuclear or conventional (torpedo)

Platform: *Los Angeles* and *Seawolf* SSNs

Remarks: As of this writing little information is available about this 1990s replacement for SUBROC. Said to be launchable from depths of over 350 ft, to follow a ballistic trajectory to its target and to drop its munitions (nuclear depth charge or Mk 46/Mk 50 torpedo) by parachute.

AIR-TO-SURFACE MISSILES

Shrike AGM-45

Length: 10 ft
Propulsion: Solid fuel
Guidance: Passive radar homing
Range: 10 nm
Warhead: Conventional
Platform: Fighter and attack aircraft
Remarks: An elderly anti-radar missile due to be replaced by HARM.

Maverick AGM-65E/F

Length: 8 ft 2 in
Propulsion: Solid fuel
Guidance: AGM-65-E laser/AGM-65F-infrared
Range: up to 50 nm
Warhead: Conventional (300 lb)
Platform: Attack aircraft
Remarks: The Marines use the AGM-65E and the Navy the AGM-65F. In a 1983 test a Maverick sank an old destroyer.

Harpoon AGM-84A

The air-launched version of Harpoon (see Surface- to-Surface Missiles). Launchable from Intruders, Orions and other aircraft and helicopters.

HARM AGM-88A

Length: 13 ft 7 in
Propulsion: Sold fuel
Guidance: Radar homing
Range: 80 nm
Warhead: Conventional (145 lb)
Platform: Fighter and attack aircraft
Remarks: A new high-speed anti-radar missile, the successor to Shrike. Approximately 8000 on order.

Marine Corps AGM Missiles

The Marines also use TOW II MGM-71 helicopter- or ground-launched optically-guided wire-controlled anti-tank missiles. They have a speed of Mach 1 and a range of 2.3 nm. A newer anti-tank missile is the Hellfire AGM-114A, which may be guided by laser, radio-frequency and infrared or infrared imaging. It is bigger and has better range than TOW.

Penguin II

A Norwegian ship-to-ship missile being considered by the Navy for launch from SH-60B helicopters. It is 9 ft long, uses inertial guidance and infrared homing and has a range of 20+ nm.

Skipper AGM-123A

A low-cost ($20,000) air-to-surface missile consisting of a Shrike motor tipped with a 1000-lb bomb and guided by an infrared seeker.

FAR LEFT: *An Intruder launches a Skipper AGM-123A, a relatively simple combination of a 1000-lb bomb, an infrared seeker and a rocket motor.*
LEFT: *The Maverick air-to-ground missile. Procurement of 1695 was authorized under FY 1986.*

ABOVE: *A Harpoon comes aboard a target ship.*

AIR-TO-AIR MISSILES

LEFT: *Sidewinder (left) and Sparrow air-to-air missiles.*
ABOVE: *The Hornet has Sidewinder stations on its wingtips.*

Sparrow III AIM-7F/M

Length: 12 ft

Propulsion: Solid fuel

Guidance: Semi-active radar homing

Range: 30 nm

Warhead: Conventional (88 lb)

Platform: Fighter aircraft

Remarks: Continuously improved since it entered service in 1976. The newest version is reported to have a speed in the order of Mach 3.5.

Sidewinder AIM-9H/L/M

Length: 9 ft 6 in

Propulsion: Solid fuel

Guidance: Infrared homing

Range: 12 nm

Warhead: Conventional (20-25 lb)

Platform: Fighter and attack aircraft

Remarks: The most widely-used air-to-air missile in the West (over 110,000 in service in 28 countries). A version called Sidearm is an anti-radar missile.

ABOVE: *A Fighter/Attack Squadron
314 Hornet launches a
Sidewinder.*

ABOVE: *A USAF F-16 Falcon test-fires the new AMRAAM (Advanced Medium-Range Air-to-Air Missile).*
LEFT: *A Tomcat with a full load of six 110-nm-range Phoenix air-to-air missiles.*

Phoenix AIM-54A/C

Length: 13 ft	
Propulsion: Solid fuel	
Guidance: Semiactive radar/active radar homing	
Range: 110 nm	
Warhead: Conventional (135 lb)	
Platform: F-14 Tomcat	

Remarks: The longest-range and most sophisticated air-to-air missile in the world. Can only be fired by the Tomcat and its AWG-9 fire-control system. About 2500 have been built.

AMRAAM AIM-120A/B/C

Length: 12 ft	
Propulsion: Solid fuel	
Guidance: Command-inertial/active radar homing (AIM-120A) or infrared homing (AIM-120B)	
Range: *c* 50 nm	
Warhead: Conventional (*c* 50 lb)	
Platform: Fighter and attack aircraft	

Remarks: This sophisticated new missile is intended to replace the Sparrow in the 1990s. Flight testing began 1984; first development models to Navy and USAF 1986. Navy requirement could be *c* 7000 units.

TORPEDOES

ABOVE: *The Mk 46 light torpedo, here carried on the side of an SH-3 Sea King, is the standard Navy air- or surface-launched ASW weapon.*
RIGHT: *A Mk 48 submarine torpedo being loaded onto SSN 650 Pargo.*

Mk 48 Heavy Torpedo

Length: 19 ft 2 in
Propulsion: Piston engine (liquid fuel)/pump-jet
Guidance: Wire guidance/active-passive acoustic homing
Range: *c* 20 nm
Speed: 50+ mph
Warhead: Conventional (650 lb)
Platform: SSNBs and SSNs
Remarks: The Navy's standard submarine-launched torpedo. Wire-guided, its performance and resistance to countermeasures is being improved via a retrofitted conversion system called ADCAP.

MK 50 Advanced Light Torpedo

Length: 9 ft 6 in
Propulsion: Stored energy propulsion system/pump-jet
Guidance: Active-passive acoustic homing
Range: ?
Speed: 50+ mph
Warhead: Conventional (*c* 100 lb)
Platform: ASW surface ships, aircraft and helicopters
Remarks: Intended as a replacement for the Mk 46 in the 1990s, it carries an AKY-14 programmable digital computer and can dive to depths of over 1900 ft.

Mk 46 Light Torpedo

Length: 8 ft 6 in
Propulsion: Piston engine (solid or liquid fuel)
Guidance: active/passive acoustic homing
Range: 4 nm
Speed: 45 mph
Warhead: Conventional (*c* 95 lb)
Platform: ASW surface ships (launched via tubes or ASROC), aircraft and helicopters, or via CAPTOR mine
Remarks: The Navy's standard surface-launched torpedo. Although extensively up-dated, it still is too short-range, too slow, too shallow-running and has too small a warhead for current ASW conditions.

MINES

Mk 52/55/56 Airdropped ASW Mines

The Mk 52 mines come in a variety of pressure, acoustic and magnetic influence versions. They carry about 625 lb of explosives and can be moored up to depths of about 160 ft. Mk 55 mines are similar to Mk 52s but carry 1200 lb of explosives. Mk 56 mines have magnetic field exploders, carry about 360 lb of explosives and can be moored up to depths of about 1000 ft.

Mk 57 Submarine-laid ASW Mine

Carries about 340 lb of explosives and can be moored in depths of 800+ feet.

Mk 60 CAPTOR

Submarine-laid or air-dropped, this ASW mine's payload is a Mk 46 torpedo, which it fires upon sensing (acoustically) the presence of a hostile submarine. It is described as a 'deep water weapon.'

Mk 65 Quickstrike

An air-dropped mine intended mainly for use against surface ships. It is a 'thin-walled' 2390-lb bomb moored at shallow continental-shelf depths (c 600 ft). Earlier Quickstrike mines include the Mk 62, based on a 500-lb bomb; the Mk 63, based on a 1000-lb bomb; and the Mk 64, based on a 2000-lb bomb.

Mk 67 SLMM

This anti-ship mine is configured like a torpedo, so that it can be launched via a submarine's torpedo tubes in order to be moored some distance away (secretly or in some area inaccessible to the submarine itself). Still in development and not expected to be available in significant quantities before the late 1980s.

ABOVE: *The P-3C Orion can carry up to six 1000-lb mines.*
LEFT: *Most attack submarines, such as those of the* Los Angeles *class, can lay mines, but the Navy uses no surface ships for this task.*

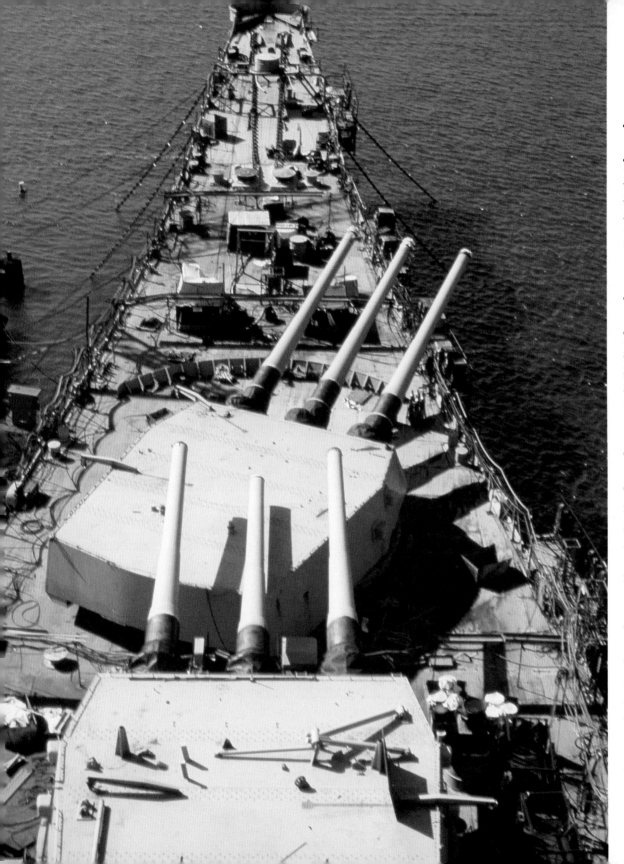

GUNS

Mk 7 16-in/50-cal

Mount: Triple turret

Range: Up to 41,622 yards

Explosive weight: Up to 2700 lb

Platform: *Iowa* class battleships
(three turrets of three guns each)

5-INCH GUNS

Mk 12 5-in/38-cal

Mount: Twin

Range: Up to 17,306 yards

Explosive weight: 55 lb

Platform: *Iowa* class battleships
(six twin mounts)

Mk 42 5-in/54-cal

Mount: Single

Range: 25,909 yards

Explosive weight: 70 lb

Platform: *Truxtun* and *Belknap* class cruisers, *Coontz* and
Adams class destroyers, *Knox* class frigates, etc.

Remarks: Mostly limited to surface targets. Remote control.

Mk 45 5-in/54-cal

Mount: Single

Range: 25,909 yards

Explosive weight: 70 lb

Platform: *Virginia*, *California* and *Ticonderoga* class
cruisers; *Arleigh Burke*, *Spruance* and *Kidd* class
destroyers; Coast Guard ships; etc.

Remarks: Air or surface targets. Remote control. Up to 20
rpm.

3-IN GUNS

Mk 21 and Mk 22 single- and twin-mounted 3-inch/50-cal guns are found on various surface combatants and auxiliaries. All are obsolete.

76-MM GUNS

Mk 75 76 mm/62-cal

Mount: Single	
Rate of fire: 85 rpm	
Range: 21,000 yards	
Explosive weight: 14 lb	
Platform: *Oliver Hazard Perry* class frigates and *Pegasus* class hydrofoil patrol boats	

40-MM GUNS

Mk 1 (in single, twin or quadruple mounts) is used on a variety of small combatants and as tertiary armament on *Iowa* class battleships. The single-mounted Mk 19 is a type of rapid-fire grenade launcher used on some auxiliaries and Coast Guard ships. The Mk 1 guns cycle at 160 rpm.

25-MM GUNS

The Mk 88 Bushmaster is a single-barrel weapon firing ammunition from a chain-linked belt. It cycles at 200 rpm.

Mk 10 and Mk 16 20-mm

The Mk 10 is a single-barrel Oerlikon with a 45-rpm cycling rate. The Mk 16 is also a single-barrel gun with an 800 rpm cycling rate and a 3300-yard range. Used on small combatants, amphibious ships and auxiliaries.

Mk 15 Phalanx 20-mm CIWS

Mount: Single, six-barrel gatling	
Rate of fire: 3000 rpm	
Range: 1625 yards	
Platform: Planned for 250 ships of all types	
Remarks: A gatling-type close-in air defense weapon now becoming standard in the fleet in one-to-four mounts per ship. Each mount has both a target-tracking radar and a fire-control radar coordinated by a computer. The non-explosive projectiles have depleted-uranium cores. Other versions of 25-mm and 30-mm may follow in the 1990s.	

LEFT: *A Mk 15 Phalanx CIWS mount. Perhaps inevitably, the Navy has unofficially nicknamed it 'R2D2.'*

FAR LEFT: *The 1700-lb 'A' and 'B' turrets of BB 61 Iowa's 16-in main battery.*

LEFT BELOW: *A Mk 45 5-in gun mount on CG 47 Ticonderoga. Behind it is a Mk 26 missile launcher.*

SENSORS

Surface-search radars

The newest surface-search/navigational radar is the solid-state C-band SPS-67. Earlier surface-search radars are the C-band SPS-10 and the X-band SPS-55. Used on surface combatants.

Two-dimensional air-search radars

One of the most widely used is the SPS-40 B-band or pulse-compression P-band radar. It is being replaced by the SPS-49 C-band and the SPS-58/65 D-band radars.

Three-dimensional air-search radars

The SPS-48 E-band or SPS-52 S-band radars are used by most large surface combatants. By far the most sophisticated 3-D air-search radars are the fixed-array SPY-1 sets now used by Aegis cruisers and being modified for carriers and *Arleigh Burke* class destroyers. SPY-1 is also capable of target-tracking and missile-guidance. It can handle nearly 20 intercepts simultaneously and can track over 250 targets up to distances of about 200 nm.

Fire-control radars

The Navy uses numerous fire-control radars, many specific to certain missiles, mounts or fire-control systems. Among the more advanced are the 20 nm-range X- band SPQ-9 used by Aegis cruisers and *Spruance* class destroyers and the X-band SPG-60, which is the Standard SM-2MR missile illuminator used on Aegis cruisers. The newest target acquisition/fire-control radar, the TAS Mk 23, can track up to 54 aerial targets simultaneously at ranges up to 90 nm. It is being added to *Spruance* class destroyers and others.

Surface ship hull-mounted sonars

The two primary hull-mounted sonars are the SQS-26 carried by most older cruisers, destroyers and frigates and the SQS-53 (an SQS-26 combined with a computer) used by *Ticonderoga* class cruisers and *Spruance*, *Kidd* and *Arleigh Burke* class destroyers.

Surface ship towed array sonars

The newest of these towed passive sonar arrays are the mile-long TACTAS SQR-18 and SQR-19 used by *Knox*, *Spruance* and *Arleigh Burke* destroyers and *Ticonderoga* class cruisers. An ultra-sensitive three-mile array, towed by T-AGOS ocean surveillance ships, is called SURTASS.

Submarine sonars

Among the newer hull-mounted sonars are the BQQ-5 active/passive systems used by SSNs and the BQQ-6 passive-only systems used by SSBNs. Submarines can also tow sonar arrays, the newest being the BQR-23 STASS system used by *Ohio* class SSBNs and *Los Angeles* class SSNs. A new under-ice sonar, the BQS-15, has been developed for *Los Angeles* class SSNs. Finally, in development for SSNs is an elaborately computerized new system called SUBACS that will combine active and passive hull-mounts and passive towed arrays. Data will be analyzed by a UYS-1 signal processor, USH-26 signal recorder and UYK-20 data processor.

ABOVE: *The eight-sided plate on the front of CG 47* Ticonderoga's *superstructure is one of the four fixed faces of the SPY-1 radar, heart of the Aegis system.*
LEFT: *An SPS-40 air-search radar on the aftermast of a* Spruance *class destroyer.*

Helicopter sonars

The two principal types of sonars that can be lowered from helicopters are the active ASQ-13 dipping sonar and the active/passive ASQ-14 towed sonar, which is used in mine countermeasures operations.

Sonobuoys

Sonobuoys can be dropped by several types of ASW airplanes and helicopters and can, depending on the type, probe actively or passively for acoustic signals to depths of *c* 1500 ft. One type, the SQQ-36, records water temperature variations up to 1000 ft. The SQQ-75, now in development, is designed to seek (actively) 'very quiet submarines.'

SOSUS

The Navy's Sound Surveillance System is a vast array of passive sonars anchored to the ocean floor along various continental shelves, 'choke points' and other strategic areas. Data from these sensors is computer-analyzed and relayed to ASW ships and aircraft.

Magnetic anomaly detectors

MAD units, which can detect the magnetic disturbances created by metal submarine hulls, are short-range (*c* 1000 ft) sensors carried by ASW aircraft and helicopters. The unit now most used is the ASQ-81(V)2.

Sensor countermeasures systems

The Navy deploys a wide array of systems to counter enemy sensors. These include such electronic radar detection/jamming devices for surface ships as the SLQ- 32 series and, for Prowler aircraft, the ALQ-92 and -99 jammers. Such systems often operate in conjunction with chaff dispensers, infrared decoys and flares. Analogous acoustic warning/jamming systems are carried by submarines or towed by ships. Predictably, a family of counter-countermeasures systems has also arisen. Few details of any of these devices are public.

LEFT: *An SH-3 Sea King lowers its ASQ-13 dipping sonar.*
BELOW: *An ASQ-81(V)2 magnetic anomaly detector deployed from an SH-2F Seasprite.*

Chapter 3
STRATEGIC MISSILE SUBMARINES

SSBN 631 Ulysses S Grant.

Strategic missile submarines (SSBNs) constitute probably the most important leg of the triad of United States strategic offensive forces. As of early 1987 this force included 28 older strategic missile submarines equipped with Poseidon C-3 or Trident C-4 missiles and nine new, much larger *Ohio* class submarines built to carry the Trident C-4 missile and eventually the D-5. The new SSBNs were being built at the rate of about one a year in the late 1980s. These are the largest submarines yet built in the United States. They are also almost certainly the most sophisticated such vessels in the world.

It is expected that the number of new SSBNs in commission will increase slowly into the 1990s, at which time the older *Lafayette* class vessels will be approaching the end of their projected service life of 30 years. The decommissioning of the older vessels could potentially bring the SSBN force as low as 15 submarines by the late 1990s, though this is not a likely eventuality.

By the end of the century the force of new Trident submarines is expected to number 20 vessels, 10 of which will operate in the Alantic out of Kings Bay, Georgia. The other 10 vessels will operate in the Pacific out of Bangor, Washington. Each new submarine will carry 24 submarine-launched ballistic missiles (SLBM). The much larger (half-again as large as the *Ohio* class) Soviet *Typhoon*-class submarines have 20 tubes. Beginning with the ninth *Ohio* class SSBN, the submarines will be equipped from the outset to fire D-5 missiles. The Trident C-4 missiles in the first eight vessels will be replaced with D-5s in the late 1980s and early 1990s. The ninth *Ohio* is SSBN 734 *Tennessee*.

SSBNs are at sea on deterrent patrol for more than half of their service lives. Since the first of these patrols began in 1960 with the USS *George Washington*, more than 2000 have been carried out. Patrols are usually of about 2-months' duration. At the present time the newer *Ohio* class Trident submarines operate in the Pacific while the older *Lafayette* class submarines patrol in the Atlantic.

SSBNs have two alternating crews designated 'blue' and 'gold.' While one crew is at sea, the other is on shore duty which consists primarily of training. During the approximately 25-day change-over period the reactor is refueled, stores are replenished and various maintenance tasks are completed.

LEFT: *SSBN 626* Ohio *receiving a Trident in a canister container.*

RIGHT: *The lower level of* Ohio's *missile compartment.*

Although the French and British nuclear submarine forces are much smaller than those of the United States and the Soviet Union, they are nevertheless a significant strategic force. Trident II missiles will be used on four new British nuclear submarines scheduled to be built over the next 10 years. France currently deploys six nuclear submarines and a seventh is scheduled for completion in 1994. The older French submarines are armed with 16 single-warhead M-20 SLBMs. The new submarine will be armed with 16 M-4 multiple-warhead missiles ($6 \times c$ 150 KT).

It has been estimated that in an all-out nuclear exchange the Anglo-French SSBNs alone would, by the 1990s, have the theoretical capacity to ruin more than half of Soviet industry.

Ohio Class Nuclear-Powered Ballistic Missile Submarines

ABOVE: *SSBN 729* Georgia.   RIGHT: *SSBN 726* Ohio.

The new *Ohio* class nuclear-powered strategic missile submarines (SSBNs) are the largest submarines yet built by a Western nation. They are the only 24-missile-tube SSBNs in the world. They can submerge to about 1000 ft. They are equipped with Mk 98 computerized missile fire-control and Mk 118 torpedo fire-control systems. A BQQ-6 passive sonar is mounted in the bow, and a BQR-15 array can be towed astern. Four torpedo tubes are located amidships.

The *Ohio*s are powered by S8G pressurized water reactors. The first American nuclear submarine, the *Nautilus*, was fitted with a PWR, for at the time it was thought that boiling water reactors were not suitable for use on submarines. Although it has since been shown that BWRs are feasible for powering submarines, the Navy has stayed with the PWR, which it knows best. In a PWR, the water is subjected to pressure of about 2000 psi so that it can be heated to operating temperature without boiling.

The *Ohio*s have turned out to be significantly quieter than expected. When the pressurized water in the reactor is moving by convection rather than pumps, the *Ohio*s may be the most quiet nuclear submarines ever built. They have a cruising endurance of about 70 days.

The first operational deployment of *Ohio* began on 1 October 1982 and continued until 10 December 1982. *Ohio* is in Submarine Squadron 17, which was established on 5 January 1981. It and the next seven boats of the class now carry Trident C-4 missiles. These will eventually be replaced with Trident D-5 missiles. All *Ohio*s have two Mk 2 SINS (Ship's Inertial Navigational System) and carry navigational satellite receivers, as well. Each has two Kollmorgen periscopes, a Type 152 and a Type 82.

The *Ohio* class submarines are an outgrowth of the Department of Defense STRAT-X study of 1967-1968 carried out to determine future strategic weapon needs. A major recommendation to emerge from this study was the building of a new class of relatively large strategic missile submarines that could carry very long-range (about 6000 nm) ballistic missiles. Proposals from Congress and the Department of Defense for constructing smaller ballistic missile submarines have

been opposed by the Navy's submarine service.

The original intent was that all submarines of this class were to be named for states. The first exception was SSBN 730, which was named *Henry M Jackson* in honor of the late senator who was a leading supporter of the Navy's nuclear vessel program.

Names: SSBN 726 *Ohio*, SSBN 727 *Michigan*, SSBN 728 *Florida*, SSBN 729 *Georgia*, SSBN 730 *Henry M Jackson*, SSBN 731 *Alabama*, SSBN 732 *Alaska*, SSBN 733 *Nevada*, SSBN 734 *Tennessee*, eight more authorized.
Displacement: 16,754 tons standard/18,750 tons submerged
Length: 560 ft
Propulsion: One S8G reactor and two steam turbines geared to a single shaft and delivering 60,000 shp.
Speed: 28 kt surface/*c* 30 kt submerged
Armament: 24 Trident C-4 or Trident D-5 ballistic missiles/ four 21-in tubes for Mk 48 torpedoes.

Lafayette and *Benjamin Franklin* Class Nuclear-Powered Ballistic Missile Submarines

Since both of these classes evolved from the earlier *Ethan Allen* class they are very similar in design. In both the pressure hulls are made of high-yield steel capable of withstanding pressures of up to 80,000 psi. The 12 *Benjamin Franklin* boats (SSBN 640-659) differ from the *Lafayette* boats (SSBN 616-636) primarily in having quieter propulsion machinery.

Originally designed to carry the Polaris A-3 missile, all units in both classes were subsequently modified to carry the Poseidon C-3. More recently, six units in each class were modified again to carry the Trident C-4. (Units so modified are marked with an asterisk in the table below).

The boats of both classes are equipped with Mk 88 missile and Mk 113 torpedo fire-control systems. BQR-7 and -21 passive sonars are carried in the hull and BQR-15 arrays can be towed astern. These boats can operate at depths up to

about 1000 ft. The sea patrol time for the approximately 130 men and 13 officers who constitute their crews is, on average, 68 days.

Unlike the *Ohios*, these boats operate only in the Atlantic. All the Trident-carrying boats are home-ported at Kings Bay, Georgia. Others operate out of New London, Connecticut, and Holy Loch, Scotland.

The *Lafayettes* and *Franklins* are all constructions of the 1960s and so will be nearing the end of their service lives in the 1990s. Some, however, will be withdrawn from service sooner, since as long as the United States continues to adhere to the provisions of SALT II at least one older SSBN must be decommissioned whenever an *Ohio* becomes operational. A typical SALT II mix for the mid-1990s might by 17 *Ohios* (408 missiles) and 19 older types (304 missiles). The upper limits, according to SALT II, should be 44 SSBNs and 710 missiles for the US and 62 SSBNs and 950 missiles for the USSR.

Names: SSBN 616 *Lafayette*, SSBN 617 *Alexander Hamilton*, SSBN 620 *John Adams*, SSBN 622 *James Monroe*, SSBN 624 *Woodrow Wilson*, SSBN 625 *Henry Clay*, SSBN 626 *Daniel Webster*, SSBN 627 *James Madison*,* SSBN 628 *Tecumseh*, SSBN 629 *Daniel Boone*,* SSBN 630 *John C Calhoun*,* SSBN 631 *Ulysses S Grant*, SSBN 632 *Von Steuben*,* SSBN 633 *Casimir Pulaski*,* SSBN 634 *Stonewall Jackson*,* SSBN 636 *Nathanael Greene*, SSBN 640 *Benjamin Franklin*,* SSBN 641 *Simon Bolivar*,* SSBN 642 *Kamehameha*, SSBN 643 *George Bancroft*,* SSBN 644 *Lewis and Clark*, SSBN 645 *James K Polk*, SSBN 654 *George C Marshall*, SSBN 655 *Henry L Stimson*,* SSBN 656 *George Washington Carver*, SSBN 657 *Francis Scott Key*,* SSBN 658 *Mariano G Vallejo*,* SSBN 659 *Will Rogers*

Displacement: 7350 tons standard/8250 tons submerged

Length: 425 ft

Propulsion: One SW5 reactor and two steam turbines geared to a single shaft and delivering 15,000 shp

Speed: 20 kt surface/25 kt submerged

Armament: 16 Poseidon C-3 or Trident C-4 ballistic missiles/four 21-in tubes for Mk 48 torpedoes

SSBN 640 Benjamin Franklin *while in port in Norfolk, Va, for a change of command ceremony.*

Chapter 4
ATTACK
SUBMARINES

An artist's impression of SSN 21
Seawolf, *leader of a new class of*
attack submarines the Navy hopes
will begin joining the fleet in
about 1995.

ABOVE: *The nuclear-powered SSNs of the* Los Angeles *class are the most advanced attack submarines now in the Navy, and probably in the world.*

philosophy and are generally conceded to be by far the most sophisticated SSNs anywhere deployed. Yet the hectic rate at which submarine and antisubmarine technology is developing has already prompted the Navy to develop an even more sophisticated class, the *Seawolfs*, which it hopes to begin adding to the fleet in the late 1990s.

As of 1987 the Navy had over 95 SSNs and four diesel-electric attack submarines in service. It had hoped to have 100 SSNs deployed by the beginning of the '90s, but whether this figure can be attained or maintained depends both on fiscal constraints and on the rate at which older boats are retired.

In addition to being able to launch torpedo and missile attacks on ships and other submarines, SSNs can now bombard land targets up to 1350 nm inland with conventional or nuclear-armed Tomahawks. They are also useful as intelligence-gatherers and minelayers. Although they normally operate alone, in wartime one or more SSNs could also be expected to give direct support to such formations as Battle Groups and Surface Action Groups. Unlike SSBNs, SSNs fall under the direct command of the several Fleets.

Seawolf Class Nuclear-Powered Attack Submarines

The newest American SSNs, the boats of the *Seawolf* class, are currently only in the planning stage. If Congress or the post-1988 Administration does not intervene, the first unit, SSN 21 *Seawolf*, will be laid down in 1989 and will be expected to enter service around 1995. There was, incidentally, a *Seawolf* (SSN 575) already in the fleet when SSN 21 was named, but she was retired in 1986.

The numeral '21' was chosen to suggest that the new *Seawolfs* will be SSNs of the twenty-first century, and indeed they are intended to surpass the current *Los Angeles* boats in nearly every department. They will be quieter, faster and deeper diving, and will have larger weapons loads and better sensors and communications. Their smaller length-to-beam ratio, the addition of retractable bow planes and six stern fins

As originally conceived, nuclear-powered attack submarines (SSNs) were intended primarily to attack both surface ships and SSBNs with torpedoes. The advent of underwater-launched cruise missiles has, however, greatly expanded their role, ranking them among the most formidable warships afloat.

Since the Soviet Navy has – and is expected to maintain – a considerable quantitative lead in both nuclear-powered and diesel-electric attack submarines, the US Navy has concentrated heavily on trying to extend its qualitative lead. At present the more than 30 nuclear-powered boats of the expanding *Los Angeles* class are the leading exemplars of this

ABOVE: *SSN 718* Honolulu (Los Angeles *class*).

and a hydrodynamically refined sail should provide for considerably improved maneuverability. The bow torpedo tubes will be enlarged from 21 to 30 in both to allow for quieter 'swim-out' of the currently used Mk 48 wire-guided homing torpedo and for larger-diameter successor torpedoes that may be developed in the future. The specifications given below are provisional.

Name: SSN 21 *Seawolf*
Displacement: *c* 9150 tons submerged
Length: *c* 325 ft
Propulsion: One pressurized water reactor. Unknown drive of about 60,000 hp. Single pump-jet type propeller.
Speed: *c* 35 kts submerged
Armament: Eight 30-in torpedo tubes forward for Mk 48; Tomahawk and Harpoon missiles; mines.

Los Angeles Class Nuclear-Powered Attack Submarines

With some 64 submarines planned by the end of the 1980s, this is the largest single class of submarines in the world. It is also the most sophisticated. These large attack submarines were developed to counter the Soviet *Victor* class of fast attack submarines. Although the *Los Angeles* class is about five kt faster than the *Sturgeon* class of the 1960s, it is still thought to be slower than the Soviet *Alfa* class attack submarines and *Oscar* class guided missile submarines.

The *Los Angeles* class boats are about half again as large as those of the *Sturgeon* class. The increased size is due primarily to the S6G reactor, which is much larger than the S5W used in the *Sturgeon* class and provides the increased speed. The *Los Angeles* class's improved sonar and fire control systems are being backfitted to *Sturgeon* submarines. Submarines from SSN 751 on have retractable control planes on the bow rather than the sail.

While both Harpoon and (eight) Tomahawk missiles can be launched from torpedo tubes in this class of submarines, only those equipped with the Mk 117 fire control system can fire the Tomahawk. Vessels from SSN 719 *Providence* on will be fitted with 12 vertical launch system (VLS) tubes for 20 Tomahawk missiles. Plans call for 33 of the 64 *Los Angeles* class submarines to be equipped with VLS. Eventually, all submarines in this class are scheduled to be fitted with the Mk 117 system and all are expected to be armed with the ASW Sea Lance Stand-off weapon that is meant to replace SUB-ROC.

All boats in the class carry UYK-7 general-purpose computers and WSC-3 satellite communications gear. Contained in their fiberglass bows is a BQQ-5 active-passive sonar. They can also deploy BQR-15 towed array passive sonars, and some are fitted with the BQS-15 under-ice set, as well. From SSN 751 *San Juan* on they will be equipped with the first generation of the Submarine Advanced Combat System (SUBACS), a new sonar-based fire-control system. Their reactor cores need replacement only every 10-13 years. In 1980 SSN 694 *Groton* was the first submarine to circumnavigate the world submerged.

As implied by the class designation, these submarines are named after cities. The naming of SSN 705 generated some controversy. Originally to be named *Chicago*, the name was changed to that of the Texas city, *Corpus Christi*. However, Catholic groups objected (Corpus Christi means 'body of Christ'), and the name was changed to *City of Corpus Christi*. Eventually SSN 721 became *Chicago*.

Name: SSN 688 *Los Angeles*, SSN 689 *Baton Rouge*, SSN 690 *Philadelphia*, SSN 691 *Memphis*, SSN 692 *Omaha*, SSN 693 *Cincinnati*, SSN 694 *Groton*, SSN 695 *Birmingham*, SSN 696 *New York City*, SSN 697 *Indianapolis*, SSN 698 *Bremerton*, SSN 699 *Jacksonville*, SSN 700 *Dallas*, SSN 701 *La Jolla*, SSN 702 *Phoenix*, SSN 703 *Boston*, SSN 704 *Baltimore*, SSN 705 *City of Corpus Christi*, SSN 706 *Albuquerque*, SSN 707 *Portsmouth*, SSN 708 *Minneapolis-Saint Paul*, SSN 709 *Hyman G Rickover*, SSN 710 *Augusta*, SSN 711 *San Francisco*, SSN 712 *Atlanta*, SSN 713 *Houston*, SSN 714 *Norfolk*, SSN 715 *Buffalo*, SSN 716 *Salt Lake City*, SSN 717 *Olympia*, SSN 718 *Honolulu*, SSN 719 *Providence*, SSN 720 *Pittsburgh*, SSN 721 *Chicago*, SSN 722 *Key West*, SSN 723 *Oklahoma City*, SSN 724 *Louisville*, SSN 725 *Helena*, SSN 750 *Newport News*, SSN 751 *San Juan*, SSN 752 *Springfield*, 17 more building or authorized.

ABOVE: *SSN 633* Hammerhead (Sturgeon *class*).

Displacement: 6200 tons standard/6900 tons submerged
Length: 360 ft
Propulsion: One S6G reactor, two steam turbines geared to one shaft and providing 35,000 shp
Speed: 30+ submerged
Armament: Harpoon and Tomahawk launched from torpedo tubes. SSN 719 and higher have 12 vertical tubes for Tomahawk. Four 21-in torpedo tubes for up to *c* 25 Mk 48. SUB-ROC, mines, etc.

Sturgeon Class Nuclear-Powered Attack Submarines

The *Sturgeons*, which were all launched between 1966 and 1974, make up the Navy's second-largest class of SSNs. They are essentially developments of the earlier *Permit* class boats, the most obvious differences being the *Sturgeons'* larger sail and a number of modifications to enhance their under-ice capabilities. The latter include sail-mounted diving planes that can rotate 90 degrees to facilitate breaking through overhead ice, strengthened sail and rudder caps and upward- and forward-looking sonars. SSN 638 *Whale* was the first of this class to conduct extended operations under the Arctic ice pack in 1969.

At present all units of the class are having their Mk 113 torpedo fire-control systems replaced by the Mk 117 so as to permit Harpoon launching. Similarly, the bow-mounted

active/passive BQQ-2 analog sonar is being replaced in the newer boats by the more capable BQQ-5 digital sonar system. Individual boats have been modified in various other ways. Some, for example, can carry small DSRV salvage submarines that can be launched and recovered while the parent submarines remain submerged. Others have altered sails that permit them to stream towed communications arrays.

Although slightly slower than the *Permits*, the *Sturgeons* are relatively deep divers, being able to operate at depths of over 1300 ft. The core life of their S5W reactors is about 5000 hours. All of them can carry up to eight Tomahawks, but only at the expense of other weapons. The *Sturgeons* operate in both the Atlantic and Pacific. They are the last class to adhere to the old Navy tradition of naming submarines for sea creatures, and even at that, three of them are named for men.

Names: SSN 637 *Sturgeon*, SSN 638 *Whale*, SSN 639 *Tautog*, SSN 646 *Grayling*, SSN 647 *Pogy*, SSN 648 *Aspro*, SSN 649 *Sunfish*, SSN 650 *Pargo*, SSN 651 *Queenfish*, SSN 652 *Puffer*, SSN 653 *Ray*, SSN 660 *Sandlance*, SSN 661 *Lapon*, SSN 662 *Gurnard*, SSN 663 *Hammerhead*, SSN 664 *Sea Devil*, SSN 665 *Guitarro*, SSN 666 *Hawkbill*, SSN 667 *Bergall*, SSN 668 *Spadefish*, SSN 669 *Seahorse*, SSN 670 *Finback*, SSN 672 *Pintado*, SSN 673 *Flying Fish*, SSN 674 *Trepang*, SSN 674 *Bluefish*, SSN 676 *Billfish*, SSN 677 *Drum*, SSN 678 *Archerfish*, SSN 679 *Silversides*, SSN 680 *William H Bates*, SSN 681 *Batfish*, SSN 683 *Tunny*, SSN 683 *Parche*, SSN 684 *Cavalla*, SSN 686 *Mendel Rivers*, SSN 687 *Richard B Russell*

Displacement: 4460 standard/4787 submerged
Length: 292 ft (SSN 678-87: 303 ft)
Propulsion: One S5W reactor and two steam turbines geared to a single shaft and producing 20,000 shp
Speed: *c* 20 kt surface/*c* 30 kt submerged
Armament: Four 21-in tubes for 15 Mk 48 torpedoes/four Harpoon/four SUBROC. Up to eight Tomahawk at the expense of other weapons. Mines.

ABOVE: SSN 612 Guardfish (Permit *class*).

Permit Class Nuclear-Powered Attack Submarines

The *Permit* class is notable in that it established the basic design features of subsequent classes of submarines. These features include deep-diving capability, large bow-mounted sonar, torpedo tubes mounted amidships and quieter machinery than its predecessors. This group of submarines was originally called the *Thresher* class. However, the lead ship (SSN 593) was lost on 10 April 1962 during deep-diving trials off the New England coast. All 112 naval personnel and 17 civilians on board perished. This tragedy was the first loss of a nuclear submarine and the worst submarine accident on record.

The *Permit* class submarines represented a major departure from earlier submarine design. They could operate at significantly greater depths than could their predecessors and were much quieter. They were also larger and slower. The large, bow-mounted sonar necessitated midships mounting of the torpedo tubes and a reduction in their number to four (two to a side, angled outboard).

An experimental direct-drive propulsion system has been installed on SSN 605 *Jack*. A large-diameter outer propeller shaft covers a smaller inner shaft. This arrangement produces counter-rotating propellers on what is essentially a single shaft. While this imaginative mechanism has reduced turbulence and has given some increase in efficiency, it has not provided an increase in speed.

Most units in the class have had their Mk 113 torpedo fire-control systems replaced with the Mk 117 system that is capable of launching Harpoon missiles. All units are also scheduled to have their BQQ-2 analog sonars replaced with digital BQQ-5s during regular refits. SSN 621 *Haddock* has tested a passive/ranging sonar consisting of six large hydrophones mounted in the hull.

The *Permits* were launched between 1961 and 1966. Eight of them operate in the Pacific, and five in the Atlantic.

Names: SSN 594 *Permit*, SSN 595 *Plunger*, SSN 596 *Barb*, SSN 603 *Pollack*, SSN 604 *Haddo*, SSN 605 *Jack*, SSN 606 *Tinosa*, SSN 607 *Dace*, SSN 612 *Guardfish*, SSN 613 *Flasher*, SSN 614 *Greenling*, SSN 615 *Gato*, SSN 621 *Haddock*
Displacement: 3750-3800 tons/4300-4600 tons submerged
Length: 278-297 ft
Propulsion: One S5W reactor and two steam turbines geared to a single shaft and producing 15,000 shp
Speed: *c* 20 kt surface/*c* 30 kt submerged
Armament: Four 21-in tubes for Mk 48 torpedoes/Harpoon/SUBROC/mines

Skipjack Class Nuclear-Powered Attack Submarines

The *Skipjack* boats represent many firsts. They were the first class to be constructed in the 'teardrop' hull configuration of the experimental *Albacore* and the first to combine nuclear propulsion and high speed. When built, they were the fastest submarines in the US Navy. Their speed was not to be equalled until the *Los Angeles* class was built. The design of the

BELOW: *SSN 585* Skipjack, *the class leader.*

Skipjack class was the basis for that of the early ballistic missile submarines of the late 1950s and 1960s. However, the tapered stern prevented installation of stern torpedo tubes. The S5W pressurized-water reactors used in this class were capable of operating 4000 hours before refueling and provided significantly increased power compared to their predecessors.

Although they were launched between 1958 and 1960, the *Skipjacks* are still considered first-line submarines, and their partisans insist that their hull design is superior to that of any subsequent American SSN. Their active/passive BQS-4 sonars and Mk 101 torpedo fire-control systems are somewhat elderly, but modifications have kept them capable. The *Skipjacks* are fitted with two electric motors that can be used to run the submarines submerged in case of reactor failure.

The *Skipjacks* are the last US submarine class whose units all begin with the same letter. All of them serve in the Atlantic. In May 1966 SSN 589 *Scorpion* and all 99 men aboard her were lost about 400 nm from the Azores.

Names: SSN 585 *Skipjack*, SSN 588 *Scamp*, SSN 590 *Sculpin*, SSN 591 *Shark*, SSN 592 *Snook*
Displacement: 3075 tons standard/3500 tons submerged
Length: 252 ft
Propulsion: One S5W reactor and two steam turbines geared to a single shaft and producing 15,000 shp
Speed: *c* 20 kt surface/30+ kt submerged
Armament: Six 21-in tubes for Mk 48 torpedoes

Ethan Allen Class Nuclear-Powered Attack Submarines

These submarines were built in the late 1950s and early 1960s as ballistic missile submarines, the first so built. They were modified later for use as attack submarines. Their service as SSBNs was limited by their lack of tactical missile capabilities, relatively large size and slow speed and low number (8) of torpedo reloads. They are now used mainly for special duties such as commando and frogmen operations.

Names: SSN 609 *Sam Houston*, SSN 611 *John C Marshall*
Displacement: 6955 tons standard/7900 tons submerged
Length: 411 ft
Propulsion: One S5W reactor and two steam turbines geared to a single shaft and producing 15,000 shp
Speed: *c* 20 kt surface/*c* 25 kt submerged
Armament: Four 21-in tubes for Mk 48 torpedoes

Other Nuclear-Powered Attack Submarines

The two remaining units of the *Skate* class still in active service, SSN 579 *Swordfish* and SSN 583 *Sargo*, both built in the late 1950s, are now considered second-line submarines and cannot be expected to remain in commission much longer. They displace 2860 tons submerged, can travel at about 20 kt submerged and have eight 21-in tubes for Mk 48 torpedoes (six forward and two aft). SSN 578 *Skate*, the now-retired class leader, was something of a trailblazer. She

passed under the North Pole twice in 1958 and surfaced nine times through the ice.

Still first-line, though one-of-a-kind, is SSN 671 *Narwhal*. Basically a lengthened *Sturgeon* (315 ft), she was designed to test a system in which a prototype reactor, the S5G, was cooled by natural circulation, thus eliminating pump noises. Her original Mk 113 torpedo fire-control system and BQQ-2 sonar have been replaced by the Mk 117 and the BQQ-5 respectively. Except for her length and displacement (5284 tons standard/5830 tons submerged), her characteristics, including armament, are similar to those of the *Sturgeons*.

The other single-ship SSN class is SSN 597 *Tullabee*, launched in 1960. She displaces 2336 tons standard and 2607 tons submerged and is 273 ft long. She runs about 15 kt on the surface and 20 kt submerged. She has four tubes amidships, angled at 10 degrees from the centerline, for Mk 48 torpedoes, and she is powered by an elderly S2C reactor. Her small hull accommodates six officers and 50 enlisted men. She still operates in the Atlantic, but is not expected to remain in service much longer.

ABOVE: *SSN 579* Swordfish (Skate class).
LEFT: *SSN 588* Scamp (Skipjack class).

Conventionally-Powered Submarines

The Navy no longer builds conventionally-powered submarines, but as of 1987 it still had five such boats on active duty, four in a combat role and one for research. The four combatant submarines were the three units of the *Barbel* class and the single unit of the *Darter* class. The research submarine was the single-ship *Dolphin* class.

SS 580 *Barbel*, SS 581 *Blueback* and SS 582 *Bonefish* were all launched in the late 1950s. Their teardrop-shaped hulls are 219 ft long and displace 2146 tons standard/2640 tons submerged. They are powered by three 1600-hp diesels, backed up by one Westinghouse electric motor, and they can travel about 12 kt on the surface and 25 kt submerged. They

have six 21-in tubes (all forward) for Mk 48 torpedoes. Two operate in the Pacific, and one in the Atlantic.

SS 576 *Darter* is the only US submarine driven by two propellers. Launched in 1956, she is slightly longer and narrower than the *Barbels*, displaces only 2250 tons submerged and can run at about 20 kt submerged. She is powered by three 1600-hp diesels, backed up by two electric motors. She has eight 21-in tubes (six forward and two aft) for Mk 48 torpedoes. Although due to have been retired in 1979, she has been retained on active duty, operating out of her home port in Sasebo, Japan.

AGSS 555 *Dolphin* is, properly, an auxiliary vessel. Filled with sensors and computers, she is used for deep-diving tests and for various acoustic and oceanographic experiments. She is 165 ft long, displaces 950 tons submerged and is unarmed. She is said to be one of the quietest submarines.

ABOVE: *AGSS 555* Dolphin, *a one-of-a-kind conventionally-powered research submarine now classed as an auxiliary.*
LEFT: *SS 580* Barbel, *the class leader.*

Chapter 5
AIRCRAFT CARRIERS

Forrestal-*class aircraft carrier CV 62* Independence. *Hers was the first class of carriers to be designed after World War II.*

With the completion of the nuclear-powered *Theodore Roosevelt* late in 1986, the Navy had 14 large carriers in service. Two more, *Abraham Lincoln* and *George Washington*, will have joined the fleet by 1991, permitting the possible retirement of the conventionally-powered *Midway* and/or *Coral Sea*, both built in the late 1940s. On 23 December 1986 Defense Secretary Caspar W Weinberger announced his intention to request funds for two additional nuclear carriers to enter fleet service in the late 1990s. If approved, these might replace the conventionally-powered *Forrestal* and/or *Saratoga*, both ships of the mid-1950s.

The Navy has stated its intention to deploy 15 carrier-centered Battle Groups by the 1990s, but as the foregoing suggests, the actual number could be slightly more or less. Much will depend, too, on the pace at which the four conventionally-powered carriers of the *Kitty Hawk* class can be put through the Service Life Extension Programs planned for them and on how long *Enterprise*'s ageing nuclear reactors can be kept going. As for actual deployability, the official norm is for big carriers to spend 12 months in overhaul, transit and local operations for every six months on station; but in fact, US carriers almost always spend much longer periods on station.

The size of US carriers has been going up steadily, from the 61,000-ton combat-load displacement of the *Midways* to the nearly 100,000-ton displacement of *Theodore Roosevelt*. Cost has been going up even faster: The two new carriers requested by Secretary Weinberger would cost in the neighborhood of $3.5 billion apiece. No one doubts that these huge ships are potent power projection/sea control weapons, but their possible vulnerability to all-out saturation attack has been persistently questioned. So far, the Navy has, on grounds of economy, resisted all proposals to spread the risk by building additional small conventionally-powered regular or V/STOL carriers for escort purposes. In fact, these would be far from cheap. Even to try to reactivate mothballed *Essex* class carriers (an unsatisfactory compromise, in any case) would cost over $500 million per ship. Yet if a supersonic, highly capable successor to the V/STOL Harrier were to emerge in the 1990s, sentiment for the construction of small carriers would doubtless intensify.

It is, however, unfair to judge the big carriers solely on the

ABOVE: *An artist's impression of CVN-65* Enterprise, *made before the world's first nuclear-powered carrier was launched.*
RIGHT: *Flightdeck crewmen direct the taxi path of an E-2 Hawkeye about to be launched from CV 41* Midway.
FAR RIGHT: *CVN 68* Nimitz.

basis of their survivability in all-out war. Ever since World War II they have repeatedly proven their worth – perhaps even indispensability – in lesser conflicts. The fact that the Soviet Navy has at last begun to build large nuclear-powered Western-style carriers is surely a recognition not only of this truth, but perhaps also a recognition that big carriers, whatever their vulnerabilities, may be essential at *all* levels of conflict. As the late Admiral Sergei Gorshkov, creator of the modern Soviet fleet, once succinctly observed, 'Seapower without air power is senseless.'

Nimitz Class Nuclear-Powered Aircraft Carriers

This class, made up of the largest warships ever built, is sub-divided into two groups. The first three ships, *Nimitz*, *Dwight D Eisenhower* and *Carl Vinson*, displace a maximum 91,600 tons. Sometimes referred to as belonging to 'the improved *Nimitz* class,' the second three, *Theodore Roosevelt*, *Abraham Lincoln* and *George Washington*, will displace about 97,000 tons, combat loaded. To the extent possible, the improvements in electronics, machinery, weapons and armor made on the newer ships will be retrofitted onto the original three. The nuclear-powered *Nimitz* class carriers all carry 90 percent more aviation fuel and 50 percent more ammunition than conventionally-powered carriers.

The Navy's first nuclear-powered carrier, *Enterprise*, was fitted with eight 35,000-hp reactors, whereas the *Nimitz* carriers have but two 140,000-hp reactors whose uranium cores need to be replaced only every 13 years. In addition to their greater efficiency, the *Nimitz*-type reactors take up much less internal space, something that is always at a premium on even the largest carriers.

At present the *Nimitz* carriers normally embark an air wing composed of 86 airplanes and helicopters. Otherwise, the ships are armed only with close-in AA weapons (intermediate-range guided missiles being – as always in Battle Groups – the special province of the escorting cruisers and destroy-

ers). All the *Nimitz* carriers have now been fitted with three eight-tube Mk 29 launchers for Sea Sparrow Missiles. These same launchers would also be able to accommodate RAMs, if and when they are adopted as Sea Sparrow replacements. The three newer ships and *Carl Vinson* also carry four Phalanx mounts; the remaining ships carry three mounts.

C13 steam catapults are fitted on all ships through *Theodore Roosevelt*, but new lower-pressure catapults are planned for *Abraham Lincoln* and *George Washington*. Many aircraft have to be parked on the flight decks, since even on these huge ships the crowded hangar decks can accommodate only about 40 percent of the total aircraft at any one time. The *Nimitz* ships carry about 15,000 tons of aircraft-related payload. Under intensive operating conditions the ships' supply of aviation fuel must be replenished every 16 days.

The ships' radar suites (at present 10 different types) are constantly being up-graded. The present SPS-10 surface-search radars will probably be replaced by SPS-67s. SPS-48s and SPS-49s are now the standard air-search equipment, and to the variety of fire-control radars the new TAS Mk 23 has

been added. A version of the SPY-1 fixed array Aegis radar will probably also be fitted. The computers in the ships' highly sophisticated ASW centers can analyze and share large quantities of target data relayed from both aircraft and the surface escorts. These carriers do not have provisions for hull-mounted sonars.

After her 1987 refit *Nimitz* will join *Carl Vinson* in the Pacific. *Dwight D Eisenhower* will be joined in the Atlantic by *Theodore Roosevelt* either later in that year or in 1988.

Names: CVN 68 *Nimitz*, CVN 69 *Dwight D Eisenhower*, CVN 70 *Carl Vinson*, CVN 71 *Theodore Roosevelt*, CVN 72 *Abraham Lincoln*, CVN 73 *George Washington*
Displacement: 81,600 tons standard/93,400 tons full load
Length: 1040 ft
Propulsion: Two A4W/A1G nuclear reactors producing a total of 280,000 shp
Speed: 30+ kt
Armament: 86 aircraft/three eight-tube Mk 29 launchers for Sea Sparrow three or four Mk 15 Phalanx CIWS

ABOVE: *CVN 69 Dwight D Eisenhower* (Nimitz *class*) *in company with CGN 36* California.
ABOVE LEFT: *An F-14 Tomcat on the deck of CVN 65* Enterprise.
FAR LEFT: *Harbor tugs edge CVN 70 Carl Vinson* (Nimitz *class*) *into a dock in Subic Bay in the Philippines.*

Enterprise Class Nuclear-powered Aircraft Carrier

Launched in 1960, *Enterprise* was the world's first nuclear-powered carrier. Although she has been extensively refitted and up-graded since then, her first-generation nuclear reactors will be 30 years old by 1990, and there is some question as to how long they can be kept in service thereafter. She can still travel about 200,000 nm between changes of her uranium fuel cores.

Enterprise at present carries 86 aircraft and helicopters. Though initially designed without defensive armament, she now mounts two eight-tube Mk 29 Sea Sparrow/RAM launchers and three Mk 15 Phalanx CIWS guns. A third Mk 29 is to be added in her next refit early in the 1990s. She has four side elevators and four steam catapults and transports enough aviation fuel to permit about 12 days of intensive air operations between replenishments.

Enterprise's radar suite (nine different types) is generally similar to that carried by the *Nimitz* ships, but the TAS Mk 23 fire-control radar will not be installed until her next refit, at which time she may also receive modified SPY-1. At that time, too, in addition to her present sophisticated ASW center, she will be fitted with a Tactical Flag Communications Center. The ship is not fitted with sonars.

Enterprise was originally assigned to the Atlantic fleet, but during the Vietnam War she was shifted to the Pacific, where she became the first nuclear-powered ship to enter combat. She has remained in the Pacific ever since.

Name: CVN 65 *Enterprise*
Displacement: 75,700 tons standard/89,600 tons full load
Length: 1040 ft
Propulsion: Two A2W reactors producing a total of 280,000 shp
Speed: 30+ kt
Armament: 86 aircraft/two eight-tube Mk 29 launchers for Sea Sparrow/three Mk 15 Phalanx CIWS

TOP: *A distant view of CVN 65*
Enterprise *passing Golden Gate.*
ABOVE: *A radar operator before his
scope in the CIC (Combat
Information Center) of* Enterprise.
LEFT: *CVN 65* Enterprise.

Kitty Hawk/John F Kennedy Class Aircraft Carriers

These four conventionally-powered carriers are generally similar in construction, although because of some variations and a slightly greater displacement (82,000 tons fully loaded), *John F Kennedy* is officially listed as belonging to a separate class. All were built in the 1960s as much-improved successors to the *Forrestal* class of the preceding decade. Now, because of their age, they are all candidates for the very extensive refits called Service Life Extension Programs (SLEPs). *Kitty Hawk*'s SLEP begins in November 1987 and probably will not be completed until mid-1990. *Constellation*'s SLEP is due to begin in December 1989, and *America*'s in the mid-1990s. No SLEP has yet been scheduled for *John F Kennedy*, the newest (1968) of the group. Meantime, they will receive constant up-gradings of equipment during their regular overhauls.

Thus it is difficult to specify exactly how these carriers will be equipped at any particular time in the near future. As of early 1987 the *Kitty Hawks* carried 86 aircraft, and *John F Kennedy* 78. All had three eight-tube Mk 29 Sea Sparrow/RAM missile launchers and three Phalanx mounts for close-in AA defence. *John F Kennedy*'s radar suite of 11 different types is the most modern, including the SPS-10F surface search, SPS-48C and -49 air-search and TAS Mk 23 fire-control equipment. The *Kitty Hawk* ships' suites will eventually be brought up to at least this standard, and all the ships may receive modified SPY-1 Aegis phased array 3D air-search radars at some point. Though *America* and *John F Kennedy* have bow sonar domes, no equipment is currently installed in them.

As of 1987 *Kitty Hawk* and *Constellation* served in the Pacific, and *America* and *John F Kennedy* in the Atlantic.

Names: CV 63 *Kitty Hawk*, CV 64 *Constellation*, CV 66 *America*, CV 67 *John F Kennedy*
Displacement: 60,100-61,000 tons standard/80,800-82,000 tons full load
Length: 990 ft
Propulsion: Four steam turbines delivering a total of 280,000 shp
Speed: 30+ kt
Armament: 78-86 aircraft/three eight-tube Mk 29 launchers for Sea Sparrow/three Mk 15 Phalanx CIWS

BELOW: *CV 67* John F Kennedy *is similar to the* Kitty Hawks *but is officially a one-ship class.*

LEFT: *CV 63* Kitty Hawk.
LEFT BELOW: *An Intruder comes on board CV 66* America (Kitty Hawk *class*).
BELOW: *CV 64* Constellation (Kitty Hawk *class*).

Forrestal Class Aircraft Carriers

The *Forrestal* ships of the 1950s were the first US Navy carriers constructed after World War II. *Forrestal, Saratoga* and *Independence* have received the major refits known as SLEPs that are intended to extend the ships' service lives 10-15 years beyond the 30 years considered normal. So far, no SLEP has been scheduled for *Ranger*, but in regular overhauls she has received three Mk 29 Sea Sparrow/RAM launchers (one more than the other ships now have) and three Mk 15 Phalanx CIWS gatling gun mounts, as well as a TAS Mk 23 fire-control radar not yet installed on the other ships. All the ships in the class will eventually be raised to at least this standard and will, in addition receive such improvements as Tactical Flag Command Centers, up-graded computers, Kevlar armor plating on vital spaces and so on.

Construction of the *Forrestals* was undertaken after the Korean War, which had decisively demonstrated the continuing importance of carrier air power and had thereby silenced the carrier's Congressional and USAF critics. The ships were originally designed to have the straight fore-and-aft decks standard at the time, but the advent of the modern angled deck caused their design to be altered while they were being built. They all have four side elevators and four steam catapults, and their 1200 watertight compartments give them remarkable watertight integrity. They can carry 5880 tons of aviation fuel (*cf* the approximately 9000 tons carried by *Theodore Roosevelt*). Their air wings are as large as those on later carriers and are similarly composed. *Ranger* operates in the Pacific, and the other three in the Atlantic.

Names: CV 59 *Forrestal*, CV 60 *Saratoga*, CV 61 *Ranger*, CV 62 *Independence*
Displacement: 60,000 tons standard/78,000 tons full load
Length: 990 ft
Propulsion: Four steam turbines delivering 260,000 shp
Speed: 33-34 kt
Armament: 86 aircraft/two or three eight-tube Mk 29 launchers for Sea Sparrow/three Mk 15 Phalanx CIWS

TOP: *CV 59* Forrestal
ABOVE: *CV 61* Ranger

Midway Class Aircraft Carriers

The three carriers of the *Midway* class were designed in World War II but entered the fleet too late to see action. They were at the time the largest warships in the Navy and were the first with beams too broad (121 ft) to permit them to pass through the Panama Canal. In the 1950s their fore-and-aft flight decks were replaced by angled decks, and all their three elevators were moved to the sides.

Despite many refits the remaining two ships in the class are nearing the end of their service lives. *Coral Sea* is due to replace *Lexington* as a training carrier in 1992, and whether *Midway* can, as the Navy hopes, remain in service until 2000 is problematic.

Since the *Midways* cannot accommodate Tomcats or Vikings, their air wings are non-standard, being composed of two Hornet fighter squadrons and two Hornet attack squadrons (a total of 48), as well as a squadron of Intruders, and detachments of Prowlers, Hawkeyes and Sea King helicopters. At present their AA armament is dissimilar: *Midway* has two eight-tube Mk 25 Sea Sparrow launchers (the Mk 25 cannot be used for RAM), and *Coral Sea* has three Mk 15 Phalanx CIWS mounts. Although *Midway* will eventually receive three Mk 15s, *Coral Sea* will probably not be fitted with missile launchers before she leaves first-line duty in 1992. The ships carry relatively modern, though not identical, radar suites composed of seven different types of radars.

Midway is the only carrier based outside the US – in Yokosuka, Japan. *Coral Sea* operates in the Atlantic.

Names: CV 41 *Midway*, CV 43 *Coral Sea*
Displacement: 51,000-52,500 tons standard/64,000 tons full load
Length: 900 ft
Propulsion: Four steam turbines delivering a total of 212,000 shp
Speed: 33 kt
Armament: 76 aircraft/*Midway* – two eight-tube Mk 25 Sea Sparrow launchers/*Coral Sea* – three Mk 15 Phalanx CIWS

ABOVE: *The flight deck of class leader CV 41* Midway *(before she received F/A-18 Hornets in her Air Wing).*

Other Aircraft Carriers

All other existing US carriers belong to the World War II *Essex/Hancock* class. Of the original 24 ships of this class only five remain, one (AVT 16 *Lexington*) on active duty as a training carrier and due to be replaced by *Coral Sea* in 1992, and the other four (CVS 12 *Hornet*, CVS 20 *Bennington*, CVS 31 *Bon Homme Richard*, CV 34 *Oriskany*) in reserve and berthed at Bremerton, Washington.

Fully loaded, these ships displace between 39,000 tons and

44,700 tons. They all have angled decks and can accommodate 70-80 aircraft, but not of the largest or most modern kind. (They cannot, for example, operate Phantoms efficiently, let alone Tomcats.) Sporadic efforts to reactivate one or another of these old ships have so far come to nothing, for they would be expensive to refit and helicopters have made them largely redundant as ASW aircraft platforms. A highly capable successor to the V/STOL Harrier might conceivably give some of them a new lease on life, but such a plane cannot be expected before the mid-1990s, when the

youngest ship of this group will be nearing 50 years of age. It is therefore more likely that any dedicated small escort carriers added to the fleet would have to be new constructions.

There is, however, another possible alternative, albeit a makeshift one. The small helicopter carriers of the Navy's amphibious force – the five ships of new *Wasp* class now being built, the five ships of the *Tarawa* class and possibly the seven ships of the old *Iwo Jima* class – might be diverted for use as small escort carriers if the right kind of V/STOL aircraft could be provided for them.

ABOVE: *CV 19* Hancock *(stricken) was the class leader for two of the four World War II carriers now in reserve.*

LEFT: *CV 43* Coral Sea (Midway *class).*

Chapter 6
BATTLESHIPS

The veteran battleship BB 62 New Jersey in 1983 after her refit prior to recommissioning.

The four units of the *Iowa* class are the only surviving battleships in the world. They all served in the Pacific in World War II and were the largest battleships ever built, with the single exception of the two gigantic Imperial Japanese Navy battleships *Yamato* and *Musashi*, which displaced nearly 72,000 tons fully loaded and mounted 18-in guns. The *Iowas*' service in the war was honorable, if not spectacular, and of the class it is perhaps BB 63 *Missouri* that is best remembered for having been the scene of the Japanese surrender in Tokyo Bay on 2 September 1945.

After the war all but *Missouri* were decommissioned, and she was relegated to serving as a training ship. The then-prevailing opinion that the day of the battleship had passed forever was, however, premature. When the Korean War broke out all four units of the class were pressed into active service and proved to be surprisingly valuable gunfire support ships. Nevertheless, when the war ended all were decommissioned.

Yet the battleships seemed to refuse to become extinct. During the Vietnam War BB 62 *New Jersey* was reactivated and again demonstrated the battleship's worth as a shore bombardment platform, serving 120 days on the 'gun line' off the Vietnamese coast and hurling her huge 16-in shells (the AP version weighs nearly a ton and a half) with deadly accuracy at inland targets up to 24 miles away. But in 1969 she was again sent back into retirement. If, in the years since World War II, battleship partisans had never quite been willing to concede that airpower had made the *Iowas*' great gun armament wholly obsolete, it seemed they must finally do so now in the age of the guided missile.

Yet the matter was less simple than it seemed. Since the late 1950s the question of whether surface ships could survive under heavy missile attack had increasingly been addressed by a race to develop ever more sophisticated AA weapons. But as the loss of the Royal Navy escorts *Sheffield* and *Coventry* in the Falklands fighting in 1982 suggested, the ability of modern warships to survive *after* they had been hit had perhaps been scanted. And in this respect the *Iowas* were, of course, matchless, for they had originally been designed for a type of warfare in which it was assumed they probably *would* be hit. No modern ships could begin to compare with their massive Class A steel armor plating. At its

ABOVE: *BB 62* New Jersey, *back in commission, fires her big guns.*
LEFT: *BB 63* Missouri *as she looked on her original shakedown cruise in August 1944.*

thickest the main armor belt on their hulls is over 12 in, and a lower belt protecting the shafts is over 13 in. Their conning towers and barbettes are even better protected, with plating more than 17 in thick, and their superimposed armored decks have a combined thickness of over 12 in. In addition, the *Iowas*' internal compartmentalization gives them superlative watertight integrity.

But what role could they play in modern naval operations? Over the years various suggestions had been put forward – to convert them to assault or 'commando' ships, complete with marines and helicopters, or to make them into hybrid battleships-cum-aircraft carriers capable of deploying V/STOL Harriers. But with the advent of the Tomahawk sentiment grew to modify them into missile platforms.

ABOVE: *BB 63 Missouri on her way to her recommissioning in 1986.*
ABOVE RIGHT: *BB 61* Iowa *launches a Harpoon.*
FAR RIGHT: *BB 61* Iowa *surrounded by small craft and with a CH-46 Sea Knight overhead.*

New Jersey was recommissioned on 28 December 1982 and was extensively modified for her new missile-launching role. She retained all nine of her 16-in rifles but lost eight of her original 20 5-in guns from the secondary battery. She was first assigned to the Western Pacific, but in September 1983 she was rushed to the Mediterranean to lend possible fire support to US Marines on shore in Lebanon. This she did only once, on 14 December, firing her 16-in guns briefly at some inland targets. *Iowa* was recommissioned on 28 April 1984 and is now operating in the Caribbean. *Missouri* began reactivation in 1984 and has been recommissioned, and funds were authorized under the FY 1986 budget for the reactivation of *Wisconsin*. (She is expected to be recommissioned in 1989.) Current plans call for these ships to become the centerpieces of four task forces called Surface Action Groups that will either operate independently or in support of carrier-centered Battle Groups.

The 32 Tomahawks carried by the *Iowas* are fired from eight four-tube elevating armored box launchers located before and aft of the after stack, and the 16 Harpoons are fired from four fixed quadruple canisters clustered about the stack itself. The ships also carry eight Super RBOC chaff launchers. Although they do not have hangars, the *Iowas* can accommodate up to four helicopters on their fantails.

The *Iowas'* extensive electronic suites typically include SPS-59 (LN-66) and SPS-67 surface-search/navigational radars, an SPS-49 two-dimensional air-search radar, SLQ-32 radar warning gear and OE-82 satellite communications equipment. All of the various weapons systems have their own fire-control systems – a Mk 38 (with Mk 13 radar) for the big guns, a Mk 37 (with Mk 25 radar) for the five-inchers etc.

There is still a good deal of debate about how survivable the *Iowas* would be in the kind of naval combat conditions that are likely to prevail by the end of the 1990s, but such questions apply equally to all surface combat types. Until such time as the matter is put to the test (with luck, never), the *Iowas* give every indication that they will go on being the fierce old survivors they always have been.

Names: BB 61 *Iowa*, BB 62 *New Jersey*, BB 63 *Missouri*, BB 64 *Wisconsin*
Displacement: 48,425 tons standard/57,500 tons full load
Length: 888 ft
Propulsion: Four steam turbines geared to four shafts and delivering 212,000 shp
Speed: 33 kt
Armament: Nine Mk 7 16-in/50-cal guns in triple mounts/12 Mk 12 5-in/38-cal dual-purpose guns in twin mounts/four Mk 15 Phalanx CIWS mounts/32 Tomahawk/16 Harpoon/up to four helicopters

Chapter 7
CRUISERS

The nuclear-powered missile cruiser CGN 36 California *in the days when she was still classed as a DLGN.*

An overhead view of the Aegis cruiser CG 47 Ticonderoga, class leader of the most sophisticated AA platforms afloat.

Ships that are called 'cruisers' today are very different from their World War II predecessors. With a main battery of 8-in guns, the old heavy cruiser was, in many respects, a smaller version of a battleship, and even until the late 1950s and early 1960s cruisers were often fleet flagships. But by the end of the 1980s *Des Moines* (CA 134) and *Salem* (CA 139) were the only old-style heavy cruisers still in existence. (They are in the Atlantic Fleet Reserve.) The main batteries of today's cruisers are missiles rather than guns, and all cruisers in active service are designed to provide AAW/ASW protection for aircraft carriers and battleships.

There have been many changes in the construction, armament and mission of the vessels called 'cruisers.' In a sense, the many changes in direction, cancellations of programs and the controversy surrounding cruisers are a reflection of the rapid changes in naval strategy and tactics that have occurred during the post-war period.

After World War II only one heavy cruiser hull – *Northampton* – intended for use as a command ship, was built, but the project was cancelled in 1945. Restarted in 1948, she was commissioned as a tactical command ship (CLC 1) in 1953. She was then changed to a national command ship (CC 1) before being stricken in 1973.

At about the same time, the classification hunter-killer cruiser (CLK) had been established by the US Navy. Originally intended for ASW against high-speed submarines, the classification was changed even before the lead ship, *Norfolk* (CLK 1), was completed. Reclassified as a frigate she was used for ASW operations until stricken in 1973.

By the end of the 1940s the Navy had all but abandoned the idea of building any new cruisers, though several wartime ships were still being modernized. Now the emphasis was on the new type of escort vessels that were to be called frigates. In 1951 the Navy established a set of designations for these new ships – DL, DLG and DLGN – and work was begun on several classes. But there remained a certain amount of confusion about how frigates were supposed to differ from the other major escort type, destroyers. In general, the frigates were larger (though not always significantly so) and were thought of primarily as AAW specialists. But by the mid-1970s there were so many overlaps in design and function between the two types that making meaningful distinctions between them was often extremely difficult.

Meanwhile, the advent of nuclear propulsion for surface ships was bringing about a gradual revival of interest in the idea of the cruiser. The Navy's first nuclear-powered surface combatant, the large guided-missile cruiser CGN 9 *Long Beach*, was commissioned in 1961, and other nuclear-powered classes followed, culminating in the four-ship *Virginia* class of the 1970s.

The re-emergence of the cruiser in some ways helped to sort out the mounting confusion about the roles of frigates and destroyers. The DL classification was abandoned in 1975, some of the larger DLs being re-designated as cruisers, while others became destroyers. The term 'frigate' (now designated FF) was thenceforth applied to a type of escort generally smaller than destroyers and specializing in ASW.

Nuclear power may have been the main reason why cruisers were revived as a type, but it certainly does not define the type today. Originally it was thought that the great recommendation for nuclear-powered missile cruisers, or CGNs,

was that they would be able to provide uninterrupted AAW escort for nuclear-powered carriers. But since Congress has failed to approve the construction of any nuclear-powered surface ships other than carriers since 1974, the Navy has perforce shifted its emphasis from CGNs to the conventionally-powered cruisers, or CGs of the *Ticonderoga* class, 27 of which are to be built by the mid-1990s. Because the *Ticonderogas* are so extraordinarily capable in other respects, and because no other surface escorts in a Battle Group would have been nuclear-powered anyway, this obligatory shift away from CGNs is perhaps less of a compromise than it might at first appear.

At present, and after much travail, the functional distinctions between the various types of escort vessels are reasonably coherent, and the cruiser's niche now seems to be well established.

CGN 9 Long Beach *before her 1980-82 modernization. She was the first nuclear-powered surface ship in the US Navy.*

Virginia Class Nuclear-Powered Guided Missile Cruisers

The four ships of the *Virginia* class, all built in the 1970s, are the newest – and probably last – nuclear-powered American cruisers. At the outset they were designated as frigates (DLGNs) but were re-christened cruisers when the DL classification was abandoned in 1975.

Their twin General Electric D2G reactors are designed to operate for 10 years between refuelings and can move the ships through the water at a flank speed of over 30 kt. The *Virginias'* weapons and electronic suites have been continuously altered and up-graded over the years, and the process is still continuing. They were, for example, originally designed with a one-helicopter hangar beneath the fantail and an elevator to bring the helicopter up on deck. This arrangement never proved very satisfactory, and with the advent of the Tomahawk sentiment grew to use the fantail, instead, as a missile platform. This conversion has already been made on CGN 41 *Arkansas*, which has exchanged helo capacity for two quadruple Tomahawk box launchers, and like modifications are planned for the others. Similarly, the Standard SM-1MR AA missiles now carried are due to be replaced with SM-2MRs, Kevlar plastic armor is being added to protect vital spaces, SPS-48C three-dimensional air-search radars are being installed to replace the older SPS-48A sets, additional CIWS gatling guns will be added and so on.

All of the *Virginias* carry SQS-53 bow-mounted active/passive sonars integrated with Mk 116 ASW fire-control systems. The missile fire-control system is a Mk 74, and the gun control a Mk 86. The *Virginias* are evenly divided between the Atlantic and Pacific fleets.

Names: CGN 38 *Virginia*, CGN 39 *Texas*, CGN 40 *Mississippi*, CGN 41 *Arkansas*
Displacement: 11,300 tons full load
Length: 585 ft
Propulsion: Two D2G reactors and two steam turbines geared to two shafts and producing 60,000 shp
Speed: 30+ kt
Armament: Two Mk 26 launchers for 68 SM-1MR and ASROC/eight Harpoon/on CGN 41, eight Tomahawk/two Mk 45 5-in/54-cal DP guns in single mounts/two Mk 15 Phalanx CIWS/six 21-in tubes for Mk 46 torpedoes

ABOVE: *Three nuclear-powered* Virginia *class cruisers. In the foreground is CGN 41* Arkansas.
RIGHT: Virginia *class cruiser CGN 40* Mississippi.

CGN 37 South Carolina (California class).

California Class Nuclear-Powered Guided Missile Cruisers

Built in the early 1970s, the *Californias* were intended to be the Navy's first major class of nuclear-powered surface combatants. But opposition by Secretary of Defense Robert McNamara and the advent of the more advanced *Virginia* design resulted in the *California* class's construction being terminated after the first two units were laid down. Like the *Virginias*, the *Californias* were classified as DLs until 1975.

The design of the *Californias* is essentially one that was proposed in the early 1960s for a class of conventionally-powered ships, and their high, somewhat cluttered superstructures betray their vintage. But since they were never intended to hangar helicopters, the addition of Tomahawk launchers is a smaller problem than on the *Virginias*, and both *Californias* are due to receive two such four-missile box launchers in the near future. Other up-gradings will include the addition of Kevlar plastic armor and the replacement of older radars with SPS-67 and SPS-49 units. Both ships have SQS-26 sonars and Mk 114 ASW fire-control systems. *California* serves in the Pacific; *South Carolina* in the Atlantic.

Names: CGN 36 *California*, CGN 37 *South Carolina*
Displacement: 10,105 tons full load
Length: 596 ft
Propulsion: Two D2Greactors and two steam turbines geared to two shafts and delivering 60,000 shp
Speed: 30+ kt
Armament: Two Mk 13 launchers and 80 SM-1MR AA missiles/eight Harpoon/eight ASROC/two 5-in/54-cal DP guns in single mounts/two Mk 15 Phalanx CIWS/four tubes for Mk 46 torpedoes

Truxtun Class Nuclear-Powered Guided Missile Cruiser

Truxtun was originally intended to be one of the conventionally-powered *Belknap* class DLG frigates, but at Congressional insistence she was given a nuclear power plant and eventually joined the fleet in 1967 as a very different, one-of-a-kind ship. She was then still classified as a DLGN, but this was changed to CGN after 1975.

She has been much modified over the years and more changes are planned. Her old 3-in/50-cal gun mounts have been replaced by two quadruple Harpoon launchers, and two Mk 15 Phalanx CIWS mounts have been added. Her present AA missile armament of 40 Standard SM-1ERs will be replaced by SM-2ERs. Two stern-mounted torpedo tubes have been removed and replaced by two dual mounts in the superstructure, and Kevlar armor and new radars have been added. With such improvements it is hoped that she can be kept in useful service through the 1990s. *Truxtun* serves in the Pacific.

Name: CGN 35 *Truxtun*
Displacement: 8,800 tons full load
Length: 564 ft
Propulsion: Two D2G reactors and two steam turbines geared to two shafts and producing 60,000 shp
Speed: 30 kt
Armament: One Mk 10 launcher and 40 SM-1ER and 20 ASROC/eight Harpoon/one Mk 42 5-in/54-cal DP gun mount/two Mk 15 Phalanx CIWS mounts/four Mk 32 tubes for Mk 46 torpedoes/one SH-2F helicopter

CGN 35 Truxtun, *a one-ship class.*

ABOVE: *CGN 25* Bainbridge, *a one-ship class.*

Bainbridge Class Nuclear-Powered Guided Missile Cruiser

Like *Truxtun*, *Bainbridge* was a one-of-a-kind nuclear derivative of a class of otherwise conventionally-powered DLG frigates, in this case, the *Leahys*. She has been progressively modernized since she entered service in 1962. Her old 3-in/50-cal and 20 mm AA guns have been replaced by quadruple Harpoon canisters, and two Mk 15 Phalanx CIWS mounts have been added. Her AA missile system has been updated to launch a total of 80 SM-2MRs, and of course her radars, sonars and fire-control systems have been steadily up-graded. But she was laid down in 1959, and how long she can be kept going into the 1990s is moot. She serves in the Pacific.

Name: CGN 25 *Bainbridge*
Displacement: 9100 tons full load
Length: 565 ft
Propulsion: Two D2G reactors and two steam turbines geared to two shafts and producing 60,000 shp.
Speed: 30 kt
Armament: Two Mk 10 launchers and 80 SM-2ER/eight Harpoon/eight ASROC/two Mk 15 Phalanx CIWS/six tubes for Mk 46 torpedoes/platform for one helicopter

Long Beach Class Nuclear-Powered Guided Missile Cruiser

Long Beach can claim an impressive list of 'firsts.' She was the first US cruiser built after World War II, the world's first nuclear-powered surface warship and the first to be equipped with guided missiles as the main battery She is also the biggest American cruiser.

Initially proposed merely as a large frigate of some 7800 tons displacement, the design was changed to take full advantage of the additional space provided by nuclear propulsion. The original guided missile light cruiser (CLGN 160) designation was changed to guided missile cruiser (CGN 160) in 1956, and she was renumbered as CGN 9 in 1957.

Long Beach was intended originally to be armed with the Regulus II strategic cruise missile. When the Regulus program was cancelled in 1958, plans were changed to have the *Long Beach* carry the Polaris SLBM. These plans were changed also, and the vessel was armed with launchers for the Terrier/Standard-ER SAM and 16 Harpoon SSMs. In 1985 armored box launchers for eight Tomahawk cruise missiles were installed. *Long Beach* operates in the Pacific.

BELOW: *CGN 9* Long Beach, *also a one-ship class.*

Name: CGN 9 *Long Beach*
Displacement: 17,100 tons full load
Length: 721 ft
Propulsion: Two C1W reactors and two steam turbines geared to two shafts and producing 80,000 shp
Speed: 30 kt
Armament: Two Mk 10 launchers and 120 SM-2ER/eight Tomahawk/16 Harpoon/eight ASROC/two Mk 30 5-in/38-cal DP single gun mounts/two Mk 15 Phalanx CIWS mounts/six tubes for Mk 46 torpedoes/platform for one helicopter

Ticonderoga Class Guided Missile Cruisers

By the mid-1990s the conventionally-powered *Ticonderogas* will constitute the largest and most sophisticated cruiser class in the fleet. The original intention was to classify them as guided missile destroyers, or DDG. The classification was subsequently changed to CG, which was felt to be more indicative of their capabilities and cost.

The *Ticonderogas* have the same hull and propulsion systems as the *Spruance* class destroyers, but there are few other similarities. New as the *Ticonderogas* are (the first entered service in 1983), the headlong pace of technological advance has already produced some marked intra-class variations. Probably the most significant pertains to armament. The first five ships in the class were equipped with two 44-missile Mk 26 launchers that could fire 68 Standard SM-2MR medium-range SAMs and 20 ASROCs. Subsequent ships are fitted with two 61-cell Mk 41 vertical launch groups that can fire Tomahawks, SM-2MRs (or newer AA missiles) and a vertical-launch version of ASROC that has about double the range of the standard ASROC. The newer ships can also operate up to two advanced SH-60B Seahawk LAMPS-III ASW helicopters, a capability that has been retrofitted on three of the original five ships, which were originally designed to carry one or two SH-2F Seasprite LAMPS-I helicopters.

Radar and sonar gear has undergone up-grading as the class enlarges. For example, CG 56 *San Jacinto*, launched in 1986, was the first in the class to get the SQQ-89 integrated ASW suite, made up of such advanced elements as the SQS-53

active/passive hull-mounted sonar, the SQR-19 passive towed array and the Mk 116 ASW fire-control system.

The currently-fitted S-band SPY-1A radar, which is the heart of the Aegis system, does not rotate. Instead, it is composed of four fixed faces (each with 4480 radiating elements) arranged at 90-degree angles to one another. It thus gives instantaneous 360-degree coverage and can provide azimuth and height search; target acquisition, classification and tracking; and command guidance to ship-launched missiles. In a real sense, its full potentialities have yet to be exploited, being limited by the capacity of the four UYK-7 computers that have to process the enormous amount of data the SPY-1 provides at ultra-high speed. The present Aegis system can nevertheless simultaneously track over 250 targets and guide nearly 20 intercepts at once.

When first proposed, the *Ticonderogas* met with the inevitable flurry of criticism. They were too cramped, too unsta-

The conventionally-powered Aegis cruiser CG 47 Ticonderoga, first of a class the navy hopes will eventually include 27 ships.

ble, too expensive, too vulnerable and so on and on. Today they are almost universally recognized as being – by a considerable margin – the most formidable AAW missile ships in the world, among the most capable of ASW ships and daunting surface-to-surface combatants.

Names: CG 47 *Ticonderoga*, CG 48 *Yorktown*, CG 49 *Vincennes*, CG 50 *Valley Forge*, CG 51 *Thomas S Gates*, CG 52 *Bunker Hill*, CG 53 *Mobile Bay*, CG 54 *Antietam*, CG 55 *Leyte Gulf*, CG 56 *San Jacinto*, CG 57 *Lake Champlain*, 16 more planned.
Displacement: 9530 tons fully loaded
Length: 529 ft
Propulsion: Four gas turbines geared to two shafts and producing 86,000 shp
Speed: 30+ kt
Armament: 68 SM-2MR and 20 ASROC *or* 122 vertically-launched Tomahawk, SM-2MR and VL-ASROC/eight Harpoon/two Mk 45 5-in/54-cal DP guns, two Mk 15 Phalanx CIWS mounts/six torpedo tubes (up to 36 Mk 46 torpedoes)/one or two SH- 2F LAMPS-I or SH-60B LAMPS-III helicopters

Belknap Class Guided Missile Cruisers

The *Belknaps*, like the slightly earlier *Leahys*, were all launched in the first half of the 1960s and were originally typed as AAW frigates until the DL classification was abandoned in 1975. A peculiarity of their design was the reinstatement of the 5-in gun, which was not carried by the *Leahys*. (The Navy had become fretful about the dwindling number of surface ships able to give fire support to troops ashore).

In 1975 the class leader, *Belknap*, was severely damaged in a collision with the carrier *John F Kennedy*, and in the course of repairs she was so extensively modified as to make her significantly different from her sisters. In another refit in the mid-1980s she was further modified to serve as Flagship of the 6th Fleet.

The other *Belknaps* have been continuously up-graded, yielding their old 3-in/50-cal guns to Harpoon canisters, receiving Mk 15 Phalanx CIWS mounts, exchanging their

Terrier AA missiles for SM-2ERs and so on. All will eventually be fitted with such advanced sensors as SPS-67 and SPS-48E radars, and all will receive the NTU (Net Threat Upgrade) modernization (which includes the Mk 14 Weapons Direction System and SYR-missile tracking set) that is also planned for the *Californias* and *Truxtun*. Five units of the class serve in the Pacific, and four in the Atlantic.

Names: CG 26 *Belknap*, CG 27 *Josephus Daniels*, CG 28 *Wainright*, CG 29 *Jouett*, CG 30 *Horne*, CG 31 *Sterett*, CG 32 *William H Standley*, CG 33 *Fox*, CG 34 *Biddle*
Displacement: 8065 tons full load (CG 26: 8575 tons)
Length: 547 ft
Propulsion: Two two-shaft steam turbines delivering 85,000 shp
Speed: 33 kt
Armament: One Mk 10 launcher and 40 SM-2ER and 20 ASROC/eight Harpoon/one Mk 42 5-in/54-cal DP single-mounted gun/two Mk 15 Phalanx CIWS mounts/six tubes for Mk 46 torpedoes/one SH-2D LAMPS-I helicopter

BELOW: *CG 30* Horne (Belknap *class*).

Leahy Class Guided Missile Cruisers

Built in the early 1960s as frigates and reclassified as cruisers in 1975, the *Leahys* were the first class of US ships to have all-missile main armament. They were also the first to feature the 'mack' superstructure, in which masts and stacks are combined into single units to conserve deck space. Their pattern of progressive modernization has been similar to that of the *Belknaps* – Harpoon canisters in place of the 3-in gun mounts, acquisition of the capacity to launch SM-2ERs, addition of Mk 15 Phalanx CIWS mounts and so on. Six of the class serve in the Pacific, and three in the Atlantic.

Names: CG 16 *Leahy*, CG 17 *Harry E Yarnell*, CG 18 *Worden*, CG 19 *Dale*, CG 20 *Richmond K Turner*, CG 21 *Gridley*, CG 22 England, CG 23 *Halsey*, CG 24 *Reeves*

Displacement: 8200 tons full load
Length: 553 ft
Propulsion: Two two-shaft steam turbines delivering 85,000 shp
Speed: 32 kt
Armament: Two Mk 10 launchers and 80 SM-2ER/eight Harpoon/16 ASROC/two Mk 15 Phalanx CIWS mounts/six tubes for Mk 46 torpedoes

CG 21 Gridley (Leahy *class*).

Other Cruisers

Only two World War II-type cruisers, CA 134 *Des Moines* and CA 139 *Salem*, have been retained in reserve for possible reactivation as fire support ships. Their main batteries consist of nine 8-in/55-cal guns in triple mounts. In addition, they carry 12 5-in/38-cal twin-mounted DP guns and 20 (*Des Moines*) or 22 (*Salem*) twin-mounted 3-in/50-cal guns.

Chapter 8
DESTROYERS

Until the Arleigh Burkes *arrive, the most potent US destroyers will remain the four* Kidd *class ships. Here, the class leader, DDG 993* Kidd.

As conceived in 1975, destroyers were supposed to function as a kind of dual-purpose type intermediate between AAW-specialist cruisers and ASW-specialist frigates. In fact, as cruisers such as the *Ticonderogas* have gained greater ASW capabilities and frigates such as the *Oliver Hazard Perrys* have gained greater AAW capabilities, these distinctions have become increasingly blurred – which should, perhaps, only be a matter of concern to the excessively tidy-minded.

In fact destroyers have great potential as an escort type, but the besetting problem of the present US destroyer fleet is age. Of those classed as guided missile destroyers (DDGs), all save the four units of the *Kidd* class are constructions of the late 1950s or early 1960s and thus will be nearing the end of their service lives in the 1990s. The 31 units of the *Spruance* class are, to be sure, constructions of the 1970s, but they were designed as standard destroyers (DDs) and were not equipped to fire any but close-in surface-to-air missiles. Of necessity, studies have recently been undertaken to see if they might possibly be given greater SAM capability in the future.

Because so many older destroyers and cruisers will be entering obsolescence in the late 1980s and early 1990s, both the Navy and the DoD have placed great emphasis on the highly capable new *Arleigh Burke* class DDGs, the first unit of which is due to enter service in 1989. But Congress has been willing to fund less than half the number proposed and has, in addition, reduced the rate at which those that have been authorized are to be built. As a result, Secretary of Defense Weinberger and others have predicted a serious shortage of AAW escort ships of all types in the 1990s.

Age has, in another way, also affected the destroyers' ASW capabilities. All the current ships save those of the *Kidd* and *Spruance* classes were designed before the extreme importance of helicopters in ASW was fully realized. As a result, only 35 of the 83 destroyers now in the fleet can carry helicopters. Luckily, the big frigate classes do have this ability.

It is clear that the future of destroyers as a type depends heavily on fundamental defense policy decisions that will have to be made by Congress and the Administration before the end of the 1980s. The ultimate fate of the *Arleigh Burkes* will thus be a kind of test case.

DD 967 Elliot, *a member of the 31-ship* Spruance *class, largest destroyer class built in the US since World War II.*

Arleigh Burke Class Guided Missile Destroyers

Since the late 1970s many people in and out of the Navy have increasingly pinned their hopes of stemming the tide of block obsolescence that will afflict the AAW escort fleet in the 1990s on two new classes: the *Ticonderoga* Aegis cruisers and the *Arleigh Burke* destroyers. Forty-nine *Burkes* were requested during the Carter Administration, and the Reagan Administration raised the number to 63. But the budget-conscious Congress, as of FY 1987, had cut the authorization to 29 and had slowed the projected annual rate of construction from five to three for the remainder of the 1980s. And undeniably the *Burkes* are an expensive proposition: The first will probably cost well over $1 billion, and the remainder around $700 million apiece.

What these sums will buy will be the world's most advanced general-purpose destroyers, equally formidable in AAW and ASW. The *Burkes* will be extremely tough ships, having all-steel superstructures and over 130 tons of armor over vital spaces. The heart of their air defense will be a modified Aegis system that includes a SPY-1D fixed-array radar linked to the five UYK-43B computers that control the AA missile load of 90 vertically-launched SM-2MRs. The *Burkes'* Mk 41 VLS system will also be able to launch Tomahawks and the longer-range VLA ASROC, and the ships will be additionally armed with eight Harpoon canisters. Gun armament will consist of two Mk 15 Phalanx mounts and one Mk 45 5-in DP mount forward. The non-ASROC torpedo armament will consist of six tubes for Mk 46s, and the ASW gear will include a hull-mounted SQS-53C sonar, a SQR-19 towed array and a Mk 116 ASW fire-control system. The ships will not have hangars, but the flight deck will accommodate one SH-60 LAMPS-III helicopter.

Despite some limitations – a comparatively modest range, a slightly less capable Aegis system than that on the *Ticonderogas*, lack of a hangar – when the first *Arleigh Burke* joins the fleet in 1989 it will be as nearly state-of-the-art as the compro-

mises inherent in any ship design allow. Yet such is the pace of modern military technology that planning for a twenty-first-century follow-on destroyer class is already under way.

An artist's concept of DDG 51 Arleigh Burke. leader of a new missile destroyer class due to begin joining the fleet in 1989.

Names: DDG 51 *Arleigh Burke*, and 28 others
Displacement: 8300 tons full load
Length: 466 ft
Propulsion: Four gas turbines geared to two shafts and delivering 80,000 shp
Speed: 30+ kt
Armament: One 64-cell and one 32-cell Mk 41 VLS launcher for 90 SM-2MR, plus Tomahawk and VLA ASROC/eight Harpoon/one 5-in/54-cal Mk 45 single-mounted DP gun/two Mk 15 Phalanx CIWS/six tubes for Mk 46 torpedoes/one SH-60 LAMPS-III helicopter

Kidd Class Guided Missile Destroyers

Until the *Burkes* arrive, the best general-purpose destroyers in the fleet will be the four units of the *Kidd* class. Oddly, these excellent ships, built by Litton/Ingalls Shipbuilding, were intended not for the American Navy, but for the Iranian. After the fall of the Shah in 1979 Congress voted the US Navy a supplemental appropriation to purchase them.

Thanks to the Iranian specifications, the ships have, among other things, exceptional air-conditioning and dust-filtration equipment that makes them especially useful for Middle-Eastern operations. They have a large helicopter hangar and were the first destroyers to have Mk 15 Phalanx mounts originally installed. Their AA missile launchers, originally designed to fire the SM-1MR, are being up-graded to handle the SM-2MR. The ASW suite, which already includes the hull mounted SQS-53 sonar and the Mk 116 fire-control system, will have a SQR-19 TACTASS towed array added, and they will receive the NTU (New Threat Up-grade) modernization and supplementary Kevlar and aluminum-alloy armor. Two *Kidds* operate in the Atlantic, and two in the Pacific.

Names: DDG 993 *Kidd*, DDG 994 *Callaghan*, DDG 995 *Scott*, DDG 996 *Chandler*
Displacement: 8140 tons full load
Length: 529 ft
Propulsion: Four gas turbines, two shafts, 80,000 shp
Speed: 30+ kt
Armament: Two Mk 26 launchers for 52 SM-1MR and 16 ASROC/eight Harpoon/two Mk 45 5-in/54-cal single-mounted DP guns/two Mk 15 Phalanx CIWS mounts/six tubes for Mk 46 torpedoes/one SH-2F LAMPS-I helicopter

Coontz Class Guided Missile Destroyers

This elderly class, all launched before 1960, began as all-gun frigates (DLs), were changed to missile frigates (DLGs) and were finally reclassified as missile destroyers in 1975. By 1977 all had been equipped to launch SM-1ER AA missiles, and Harpoon launchers were put in the places formerly occupied by their 3-in gun mounts. It was found that they were too aged, and their superstructures too crowded, to permit the installation of Phalanx CIWS guns, so their remaining armament is confined to a 5-in DP gun, ASROCs, torpedoes and machine guns. On a trial basis DDG 42 *Mahan* was fitted with NTU (New Threat Up-grade) modification intended to reduce reaction time to missile attack and was given the capability to launch SM-2ERs, but these improvements are not planned for the other ships. Whether the *Coontz* ships can remain in service through the 1990s is unclear.

Names: DDG 37 *Farragut*, DDG 38 *Luce*, DDG 39 *Macdonough*, DDG 40 *Coontz*, DDG 41 *King*, DDG 42 *Mahan*, DDG 43 *Dahlgren*, DDG 44 *William V Pratt*, DDG 45 *Dewey*, DDG 46 *Preble*
Displacement: 5800 tons full load
Length: 513 ft
Propulsion: Two steam turbines geared to two shafts and producing 85,000 shp
Speed: 33 kt
Armament: One Mk 10 launcher and 40 SM-1ER/eight Harpoon/eight-tube ASROC launcher/one 5-in/54-cal Mk 42 single-mounted DP gun/six tubes for Mk 46 torpedoes/helicopter landing pad

LEFT: *DDG 996* Chandler (*Kidd class*).
BELOW: *DDG 46* Preble (*Coontz class*).

Charles F Adams Class Guided Missile Destroyers

These relatively small vessels constituted the largest class of missile-armed surface warships in the fleet before the FFG 7 frigate class was commissioned. The first eight ships were authorized as ASW missile destroyers in 1956.

Extensive modernization plans for the *Adams* class were drawn up by the Navy for implementation in fiscal 1980. Congress, however, expressed more interest in building new destroyer-type vessels rather than rebuilding older ones, and the modernization program was severely cut back to include only three ships, DDG 19 *Tattnal*, DDG 20 *Goldsborough* and DDG 22 *Benjamin Stoddert*. The modernization related primarily to a major improvement in the ships' radars and fire-control systems. Piecemeal improvement have been made in the other ships during regular overhauls, the result being a number of intra-class variations (eg, some ships carry four Harpoons, others six; four ships mount SQQ-23 sonars, the rest have the older SQS-23). None of the ships is or will be fitted with Mk 15 Phalanx CIWS mounts.

ABOVE: *DDG 2* Charles F Adams, *class leader*.

RIGHT: *DDG 21* Cochrane (Adams *class*).

Like the *Coontz* class, the *Adams* ships, all of which were launched between 1957 and 1963, will be close to block obsolescence in the early 1990s. Eleven of the class serve in the Atlantic, the others in the Pacific.

Names: DDG 2 *Charles F Adams*, DDG 3 *John King*, DDG 4 *Lawrence*, DDG 5 *Claude V Ricketts*, DDG 6 *Barney*, DDG 7 *Henry B Wilson*, DDG 8 *Lynde McCormick*, DDG 9 *Towers*, DDG 10 *Sampson*, DDG 11 *Sellers*, DDG 12 *Robison*, DDG 13 *Hoel*, DDG 14 *Buchanan*, DDG 15 *Berkeley*, DDG 16 *Joseph Strauss*, DDG 17 *Conyngham*, DDG 18 *Semmes*, DDG 19 *Tattnal*, DDG 20 *Goldsborough*, DDG 21 *Cochrane*, DDG 22 *Benjamin Stoddert*, DDG 23 *Richard E Byrd*, DDG 24 *Waddell*

Displacement: 4500 tons full load
Length: 420 ft
Propulsion: Two steam turbines, two shafts, 70,000 shp
Speed: 31 kt
Armament: One Mk 11 or Mk 13 launcher for four or six Harpoon and 34 or 36 SM-1MR/eight or 12 ASROC/two 5-in/54-cal Mk 42 single-mounted DP guns/six tubes for Mk 46 torpedoes/helicopter pad

Spruance Class Destroyers

The *Spruance* ships both make up the largest destroyer class built in the West since the end of World War II and are the only non-SAM destroyers ordered by the Navy since the 1950s. They were built (throughout the 1970s and into the early 1980s) to replace the obsolete World War II *Sumner* and *Gearing* classes. They were the first surface combatants to be fitted with gas turbine propulsion, and their excellent basic hull design has also been used for the *Ticonderoga* class Aegis cruisers and the *Kidd* class missile destroyers.

Since they were intended primarily for ASW, the *Spruances*' AA capabilities were largely limited to close-in self-protection. At first this function was centered on a single eight-tube Mk 29 Sea Sparrow launcher, but now all ships in the class are being back-fitted with two Mk 15 Phalanx CIWS mounts, and experiments have been conducted both with a new 30-mm gatling gun and extended-range Sea Sparrows.

The advent of the Tomahawk has considerably changed the complexion of the *Spruances*' armament. Plans now call for eight ships to receive two four-tube Tomahawk armored box launchers and for the remainder to be fitted with Mk 41 vertical launch groups capable of firing up to 30 Tomahawks or VLA ASROCs. These vertical launchers could be harbingers of important future conversions to a genuine SAM-launch capacity for the class. Obviously the Navy, faced with a looming shortage of AAW escorts in the 1990s, has this much on its mind. The main problem with such a conversion is the *Spruances*' lack of appropriate missile fire-control, but conceivably this might be supplied by accompanying guided missile ships, especially those equipped with Aegis.

In keeping with their primary ASW mission the *Spruances* were designed with hangars for an SH-2F LAMPS-I ASW helicopter, and these are gradually being modified to accommodate the SH-60F LAMPS-III. Other ASW gear includes SQS-53 bow-mounted sonars and Mk 116 ASW fire-control systems. To this, SQR-19 towed arrays are to be added, and eventually all these elements may be combined in the sophisticated new SQQ-89 integrated ASW system.

Sixteen *Spruances* operate in the Atlantic, and the remainder in the Pacific.

Note: From the foregoing comments it will be obvious to the reader that the armament, equipment and perhaps even mission of the *Spruances* is in a state of flux. The armaments specifications given below (essentially the status of the majority of the *Spruances* in the mid-1980s) will probably not hold true much longer and should not be taken as representative of what the class's weaponry will be like in the 1990s.

Names: DD 963 *Spruance*, DD 964 *Paul K Foster*, DD 965 *Kinkaid*, DD 966 *Hewitt*, DD 967 *Elliot*, DD 968 *Arthur W Radford*, DD 969 *Peterson*, DD 970 *Caron*, DD 971 *David R Ray*, DD 972 *Oldendorf*, DD 973 *John Young*, DD 974 *Comte de Grasse*, DD 975 *O'Brien*, DD 976 *Merrill*, DD 977 *Briscoe*, DD 978 *Stump*, DD 979 *Conolly*, DD 980 *Moosbrugger*, DD 981 *John Hancock*, DD 982 *Nicholson*, DD 983 *John Rodgers*, DD 984 *Leftwich*, DD 985 *Cushing*, DD 986 *Harry W Hill*, DD 987 *O'Bannon*, DD 988 *Thorn*, DD 989 *Deyo*, DD 990 *Ingersoll*, DD 991 *Fife*, DD 992 *Fletcher*, DD 993 *Hayler*
Displacement: 7800 tons full load
Length: 563 ft
Propulsion: Four gas turbines geared to two shafts and producing 80,000 shp
Speed: 30+ kt
Armament: One Mk 29 launcher for 24 Sea Sparrow/eight Harpoon/24 ASROC/two 5-in/54-cal Mk 45 single-mounted DP guns/two Mk 15 Phalanx CIWS mounts/six tubes for Mk 46 torpedoes/one SH-2F or SH-60B helicopter

Other Destroyers

All four of the *Decatur* class (ex-*Forrest Sherman* class) guided missile destroyers and 10 of the 11 *Forrest Sherman* class destroyers had been retired from active service as of 1987, the remaining *Forrest Sherman* (DD 946 *Edson*) being used as a training ship. All are constructions of the 1950s. Some will continue to be kept in reserve for possible reactivation as fire support ships.

RIGHT: *DD 970 Caron (Spruance class).*

INSET: *DD 963 Spruance, class leader.*

Chapter 9
FRIGATES

The missile frigate FFG 7 Oliver Hazard Perry is the leader of the largest single class of US warships – and also one of the most controversial. She has since received a Phalanx mount.

The ships that are today classified as frigates are the descendants of the destroyer escort of World War II, ships smaller than destroyers and specializing in ASW. By the 1950s such ships were being called 'ocean escorts,' and the newly-revived term 'frigate' was being used for a larger type of ship that fell somewhere between cruisers and destroyers. Eventually, on 30 June 1975, the nomenclature was revised, producing three basic types of escorts: cruisers, which were supposed to be mainly AAW specialists; frigates, which were to be ASW specialists; and destroyers, which were supposed to be a bit of both. Over the years, however, the frigates' AA capacity gradually began to increase, as did the cruisers' ASW capacity, so that now the distinctions between the three types, though still valid in general, are less clear.

By the beginning of 1988 it is expected that the active US frigate fleet will number about 89 ships, mostly divided between the two large *Perry* and *Knox* classes, plus 24 more *Perry* and *Knox* ships that will be assigned to the Naval Reserve Force. No additional frigates will be built in the 1980s, but conceptual studies for a new frigate class that might be built in the 1990s have been undertaken.

Only two of the current frigate classes, the 51 *Perrys* and the six *Brookes* are capable of launching SAMs, and since the *Brookes* were in any case built in the early to mid-1960s and will near the end of their service lives in the mid-1990s, the *Perrys* in effect stand alone, almost as a separate type. But in large measure, the whole future of the frigate concept will probably depend on how these controversial ships are evaluated in service. Critics' objections that they may not be able to provide convoys, Battle Groups or Surface Action Groups with really useful escort in 'high-threat environments' (*ie*, when under heavy combined submarine and air attack) have become somewhat more muted of late, but doubts still remain. And the question is hardly academic, for in terms of units, the ubiquitous *Perrys* may constitute up to 30 percent of the *total* US escort fleet by the mid-1990s.

LEFT: *FFG 42* Kalkring (Perry *class*).
RIGHT ABOVE: *FFG 16* Clifton Sprague (Perry *class*).
RIGHT BELOW: *FFG 7* Oliver Hazard Perry, *the class leader*.

Oliver Hazard Perry Class Guided Missile Frigates

The construction of the *Perrys* spans roughly the decade between the mid-1970s and the mid-1980s. They are now the largest single class of warships in the world. (The Soviet *Skoryy* class of destroyers, built in the 1950s, was larger, but all these ships have now either been stricken or placed in reserve.) At one time it was proposed that a grand total of 75 *Perrys* be built, but a return of sanity, coupled with Congressional parsimony, gradually whittled the number down, and by the time Congress authorized the 51st and final unit of the class in 1984 it was over Navy objections.

One reason why the *Perrys* could be mass-produced with relative economy was their unique pre-fab form of construction. All major components were built and tested separately and were then assembled as modules that made up the final structure. The emphasis was on simplicity, austerity and low cost, for from the outset it was assumed that in many combat situations the *Perrys* would have to depend on outside support.

In the final design the *Perrys* were given side-by-side hangars for two LAMPS-III helicopters, but not all have been fully equipped to handle the complex LAMPS-III system, and in any case the rate of production of SH-60Bs has been so slow that most *Perrys* will probably not be able to operate more than one helicopter before the mid-1990s. This could sharply limit their ASW capability, since they are the only US escort ships built in the past 20 years that are not fitted with ASROC.

Their sonar gear, too, is relatively modest. For reasons of economy they were fitted with the medium-frequency hull-mounted SQS-56 rather than the well-proven low-frequency SQS-26. SQR-19 towed arrays are to be back-fitted on FFG-36-42 and FFG-45-61.

On the other hand, their AA armament is, at least in comparison to the earlier *Brooke* class of guided missile frigates, fairly substantial. Their Mk 13 launchers can accommodate

up to 40 SM-1MRs (or 36 if four Harpoons are carried), they are being back-fitted with a Mk 15 Phalanx mount and their single 76-mm OTO Melara DP guns have a fair close-in AA capability. Their AA fire-control is generally good but cannot be linked to that of other ships.

The *Perrys'* obvious limitations have made them the object of much criticism, but then they were designed to be limited in function. With the improvements planned for them, they may still prove to be valuable additions to the fleet of the 1990s. When the final unit of the class enters service at the end of 1988 the *Perrys* will probably be about evenly divided between the Atlantic and Pacific. The fact that there are no plans for a class to succeed the *Perrys* is symptomatic of a widespread feeling that the US now has a surplus of frigates.

Names: FFG 7 *Oliver Hazard Perry*, FFG 8 *McInerney*, FFG 9 *Wadsworth*, FFG 10 *Duncan*, FFG 11 *Clark*, FFG 12 *George Philip*, FFG 13 *Samuel Eliot Morison*, FFG 14 *John H Sides*, FFG 15 *Estocin*, FFG 16 *Clifton Sprague*, FFG 19 *John A Moore*, FFG 20 *Antrim*, FFG 21 *Flatley*, FFG 22 *Fahrion*, FFG 23 *Lewis B Puller*, FFG 24 *Jack Williams*, FFG 25 *Copeland*, FFG 26 *Gallery*, FFG 27 *Mahlon S Tisdale*, FFG 28 *Boone*, FFG 29 *Stephen W Groves*, FFG 30 *Reid*, FFG 31 *Stark*, FFG 32 *John L Hall*, FFG 33 *Jarrett*, FFG 34 *Aubrey Fitch*, FFG 36 *Underwood*, FFG 37 *Crommelin*, FFG 38 *Curts*, FFG 39 *Doyle*, FFG 40 *Halyburton*, FFG 41 *McClusky*, FFG 42 *Kalkring*, FFG 43 *Thach*, FFG 45 *De Wert*, FFG 46 *Rentz*, FFG 47 *Nicholas*, FFG 48 *Vandegrift*, FFG 49 *Robert E Beadley*, FFG 50 *Jesse L Taylor*, FFG 51 *Gary*, FFG 52 *Carr*, FFG 53 *Hawes*, FFG 54 *Ford*, FFG 55 *Elrod*, FFG 56 *Simpson*, FFG 57 *Reuben James*, FFG 58 *Samuel B Roberts*, FFG 59 *Kauffman*, FFG 60 *Rodney M Davis*, FFG 61 *Ingraham*

Note: FFG 7, FFG 9-23, FFG 25 and FFG 27 to the NRF by January 1988
Displacement: 3650 tons full load
Length: 445 ft
Propulsion: Two gas turbines delivering 40,000 shp
Speed: 28+ kt
Armament: One Mk 13 launcher and four Harpoon and 36 SM-1MR/one 76 mm Mk 75 OTO Melara DP gun/one Mk 15 Phalanx CIWS mount/six tubes for Mk 46 torpedoes/one or two SH-2F LAMPS-I or SH-60B LAMPS-III helicopters

Brooke Class Guided Missile Frigates

The six ships of the *Brooke* class, built in the 1960s, began their service lives as missile ocean escort ships, or DEGs, and were redesignated as FFGs in 1975. They are essentially *Garcia* class frigates in which the aft 5-in gun has been replaced by a Mk 22 launcher for 16 SM-1MR AA missiles. They also have a telescoping hangar for a LAMPS-I helicopter.

Although FFG 4 *Talbot* was outfitted to evaluate weapons and equipment to be installed on the *Perry* class, it was later restored to its original state. In fact, relatively little is planned to up-grade these elderly ships. They will not, for example, be given either Harpoons or Mk 15 Phalanx mounts, nor will they be fitted with SQR-19 towed sonar arrays. On the other hand, they do have ASROC, which the *Perrys* lack, and on FFG 4-6 these have reload magazines.

Whether the *Brookes* can continue in service through the 1990s is doubtful. The class is now evenly divided between the Atlantic and Pacific.

Names: FFG 1 *Brooke*, FFG 2 *Ramsey*, FFG 3 *Schofield*, FFG 4 *Talbot*, FFG 5 *Richard L Page*, FFG 6 *Julius A Furer*
Displacement: 3245 tons full load
Length: 390 ft
Propulsion: Two steam turbines geared to one shaft and producing 35,000 shp
Speed: 27 kt
Armament: One Mk 22 launcher and 16 SM-1MR/one eight-tube ASROC launcher/one 5-in/38-cal Mk 30 single-mounted DP gun/six tubes for Mk 46 torpedoes/one SH-2F LAMPS-I helicopter

BELOW: *FFG 1* Brooke, *the class leader.*

Knox Class Frigates

Now making up the Navy's second largest ship class, the 46 *Knox* frigates were all launched between 1966 and 1973. Despite some early design and equipment problems, progressive improvements have made them into capable ASW ships, and the modification of their ASROC launchers to accept Harpoons has given them an extra dimension as escort ships.

All but FF 1084-1097 were fitted with Mk 25 Sea Sparrow launchers for close-in AA defense, but these will be replaced by a single Mk 15 Phalanx CIWS mount by 1990. Other improvements will include the addition of SQR-18 towed sonar arrays, the installation of the new ASW TDS (Tactical Data System) and up-graded radars and electronics suites.

As originally designed, all the ships had large telescoping hangars that can accommodate a LAMPS-I helicopter, and they are fitted with bow-mounted SQS-26 sonars and Mk 114 ASW fire-control systems. Their hulls are equipped with anti-rolling fin stabilizers and with the Prairie-Masker bubble system to lower their acoustical signature.

By 1988 eight ships of the class will have been transferred to the Naval Reserve Force. Those remaining in active service will be about equally divided between the Atlantic and Pacific.

Names: FF 1052 *Knox*, FF 1053 *Roark*, FF 1054 *Gray*, FF 1055 *Hepburn*, FF 1056 *Connole*, FF 1057 *Rathburne*, FF 1058 *Meyercord*, FF 1059 *William S Sims*, FF 1060 *Lang*, FF 1061 *Patterson*, FF 1062 *Whipple*, FF 1063 *Reasoner*, FF 1064 *Lockwood*, FF 1065 *Stein*, FF 1066 *Marvin Shields*, FF 1067 *Francis Hammond*, FF 1068 *Vreeland*, FF 1069 *Bagley*, FF 1070 *Downes*, FF 1071 *Badger*, FF 1072 *Blakely*, FF 1073 *Robert E Peary*, FF 1074 *Harold E Holt*, FF 1075 *Trippe*, FF 1076 *Fanning*, FF 1077 *Ouellet*, FF 1078 *Joseph Hewes*, FF 1079 *Bowen*, FF 1080 *Paul*, FF 1081 *Aylwin*, FF 1082 *Elmer Montgomery*, FF 1083 *Cook*, FF 1084 *McCandless*, FF 1085 *Donald B Beary*, FF 1086 *Brewton*, FF 1087 *Kirk*, FF 1088 *Barbey*, FF 1089 *Jesse L Brown*, FF 1090 *Ainsworth*, FF 1091 *Miller*, FF 1092 *Thomas C Hart*, FF 1093 *Capodanno*, FF 1094 *Pharris*, FF 1095 *Truett*, FF 1096 *Valdez*, FF 1097 *Moinester*

Note: FF 1053, 1054, 1058, 1060, 1061, 1072, 1091 and 1096 to the NRF by January 1988.

Displacement: 4100 tons full load
Length: 415 ft
Propulsion: Two steam turbines, one shaft, 35,000 shp
Speed: 27+ kt
Armament: Four Harpoon/one eight-tube (reloadable) ASROC launcher/one 5-in/54-cal single-mounted Mk 42 DP gun/one Mk 15 Phalanx or one eight-tube Mk 25 Sea Sparrow launcher/four tubes for Mk 46 torpedoes/one SH-2F LAMPS-I

ABOVE: *FF 1065* Stein (Knox *class*).
RIGHT: *FF 1066* Marvin Shields (Knox *class*).

Garcia Class Frigates

Launched between 1963 and 1965, the 10 *Garcias* are similar to the *Brookes* but have a second 5-in gun aft instead of a Mk 22 AA missile launcher. They have the same vertical boilers and pressurized combustion system and the same excellent sea-keeping qualities (in part due to their anti-rolling fin stabilizers). Two ships, FF 1040 *Garcia* and FF 1043 *McDonnell*, do not carry SH-2F LAMPS-I helicopters in their hangars but are instead fitted to stream BQR-15 towed array hydrophones. Two others (now in reserve) also do not carry helicopters. FF 1047 *Voge* and all subsequent ships have ASROC reload magazines. All ships have SQS-26 hull-mounted sonars and Mk 114 ASW fire-control systems. The ships are evenly divided between the Atlantic and Pacific.

Names: FF 1040 *Garcia*, FF 1041 *Bradley*, FF 1043 *Edward McDonnell*, FF 1044 *Brumby*, FF 1045 *Davidson*, FF 1047 *Voge*, FF 1048 *Sample*, FF 1049 *Koelsh*, FF 1050 *Albert David*, FF 1051 *O'Callahan*.

Displacement: 3560 tons full load

Length: 390 ft

Propulsion: Two steam turbines, one shaft, 35,000 shp

Speed: 27 kt

Armament: One reloadable eight-tube Mk 16 ASROC launcher/two 5- in/38-cal single-mounted Mk 30 DP gun/six tubes for Mk 46 torpedoes/one SH-2F LAMPS-I helicopter (on six ships)

Glover Experimental Escort Ship/Frigate

Glover is basically a *Garcia* class ship that was detached from the class and used as an experimental ASW escort ship (AGFF) until she was returned to operational frigate duty in 1979, at which time she was redesignated FF 1098. She differs from the other *Garcias* mainly in having no after 5-in mount and in having had a pump-jet propeller installed. Her ASROC does not have a reload magazine.

Bronstein Class Frigates

The *Bronstein*s, built in the early 1960s, were the prototypes of the ocean escort vessels that have since been designated as frigates. It soon became apparent the design of the *Bronsteins* fell short of what the Navy felt it needed in an ASW escort: They were too slow, had too short a range and were indifferent seakeepers. They are today the only US frigates that still mount 3-in guns. Originally they had two dual 3-in mounts, but the after mount was removed to permit them to stream SQR-15 towed arrays. They have a Mk 114 ASW fire-control system, and their ASROC launchers are not reloadable. *Bronstein* serves in the Atlantic, *McCloy* in the Pacific.

Names: FF 1037 *Bronstein*, FF 1038 *McCloy*
Displacement: 2650 tons full load
Length: 350 ft
Propulsion: Two steam turbines geared to one shaft and producing 20,000 shp
Speed: 24 kt
Armament: One eight-tube ASROC launcher/one 3-in/50-cal dual- mounted Mk 33 AA gun/six tubes for Mk 46 torpedoes

FF 1038 McCloy (Bronstein *class*).

Chapter 10
AMPHIBIOUS SHIPS, CRAFT AND VEHICLES

The tank landing ship LST 1193
Fairfax County *(foreground) and*
the amphibious assault helicopter
carrier LPH 12 Inchon.

The Navy's amphibious force is currently in a phase of rapid modernization. By the 1990s it should have the world's most advanced capability for conducting highspeed assaults on enemy beaches from, as Navy jargon has it, OTH, or over the horizon. The basis for this capability lies in a congeries of technical innovations now in the process of development and integration. These innovations particularly affect three categories of weapons systems: assault ships, aircraft and landing craft.

The most versatile of the new assault ships, such as those of the *Wasp, Tarawa* and *Iwo Jima* classes, combine the features of small aircraft carriers, transports and floating docks that can service fast landing craft. Other ships, such as those of the *Whidbey Island* class, have the second and third features but have more limited aerial capabilities. The aircraft these ships deploy can be heavy-lift helicopters, such as the new Super Stallion that can ferry 56 fully equipped troops or 600 tons of cargo over 200 nm at better than 175 mph; the even newer tilt-rotor Osprey airplane that can ferry somewhat smaller loads over the same distance at nearly 450 mph; or V/STOL attack aircraft such as the Harrier or its eventual successor. The landing craft the ships carry may be either conventional in design or the extraordinary new air-cushion LCACs that can ferry 250 troops 200 nm at 50 kt (58 mph) and can skim over four-foot-high solid obstacles.

What these assembled technologies mean in practice is that in the near future a sizeable Marine assault force could be launched from well over the horizon and be on an enemy beach within 30 minutes – probably too short a time for the defending forces to mobilize effectively.

At present the Navy's active amphibious force consists of about 60 ships, enough to lift the assault echelon of one 48,000-man Marine Amphibious Force. (The other two echelons, the follow-on echelon and the fly-in echelon, would follow later.) The Navy hopes to expand this core force to 75-80 ships by the mid-1990s, giving it the ability to lift the assault echelon of an additional 15,000-man Marine Amphibious Brigade.

The 60-odd ships now assigned to the active amphibious force are by no means the only ships that might potentially be allocated to amphibious operations on short notice. Battleships, command ships, aviation logistics support ships, Mari-

LEFT: 'Jeff B,' the prototype test vehicle for the air-cushion LCAC landing craft, approaches the docking well of dock landing ship LSD 32 Spiegel Grove.

RIGHT: In the foreground is 3PD 11 Coronado *(since redesignated an auxiliary command ship). To the rear, right, is LPH 12* Inchon *and, left, LST 1173* Suffolk County *(now in reserve).*

RIGHT: A Harrier takes off from the deck of LHA 4 Nassau.

time Prepositioning ships and a number of older amphibious ships in the Ready Reserve could all be added to the core force, bringing the total close to 100. But this would not contribute to the force's over-the-horizon capability, and in any case, concentrating the whole force quickly could be a problem, since it is now scattered among the four Fleets in the Atlantic, Pacific and Mediterranean (and in the case of Maritime Prepositioning Squadron 2, in the Indian Ocean). This dispersion is to some extent also true of the core force.

Even without addressing the problem of dispersion, the Navy estimates that, given the projected retirement of older ships, to bring the core of the active amphibious force to a state in which it could lift both a fast-striking Marine Amphibious Force and a Marine Amphibious Brigade would require the construction of at least five 40,000-ton *Wasp* and 14 15,000-ton *Whidbey Island* class ships by the mid-1990s. And this of course will be expensive. Thus whether the amphibious potential that new technologies have made available to the Navy will be fully realized is very much at the mercy of fiscal constraints and future national policy decisions.

An artist's concept of LHD 1 Wasp, *leader of a new class of amphibious assault ships due to begin joining the fleet in 1989. Note the Harriers and LCACs.*

Wasp Class Amphibious Assault Ships

The first two units, *Wasp* and *Essex*, of this most advanced class of amphibious assault ships are currently under construction. The Navy originally wanted at least 11 *Wasp* ships, but as of 1987 it appeared that Congress might not fund more than five. *Wasp* is due to enter service in 1989, and *Essex* in mid-1991.

The *Wasp* ships are in some ways similar to those of the earlier *Tarawa* class, but they are specifically designed both to be able to carry the new air-cushion LCAC landing craft (three can be accommodated in the ships' docking wells) and to be able to carry a larger number of Harriers, should the ships be called upon to serve in the role of V/STOL carriers.

In their assault mode the *Wasps* can carry up to 2000 troops, three LCACs or 12 LCMs, and the equivalent of 46 Sea

Knight troop-carrying helicopters and six Harriers. They have 22,900 sq ft of space for vehicle parking, 109,000 cu ft of space for dry cargo and their medical facilities include six operating rooms and beds for 600 patients. In their V/STOL carrier mode the *Wasps* can accommodate 20 Harriers and four Seahawk LAMPS-III helicopters.

For AA defense they carry two eight-tube Mk 29 Sea Sparrow/RAM missile launchers and three Phalanx gatling gun mounts. Their eight types of radar include the new SPS-67 navigation/surface-search and TAS Mk 23 fire-control sets. Their 6200-ton fuel storage capacity gives them a cruising range of about 9500 nm between replenishments.

Names: LHD 1 *Wasp*, LHD 2 *Essex*, up to nine more planned
Displacement: 40,500 tons fully loaded
Length: 779 ft
Propulsion: Two steam turbines delivering 70,000 shp
Speed: 24 kt
Combat load: Assault mode: 2000 troops/equivalent of three LCACs or 12 LCMs/c 30 CH-53 or   CH-46 helicopters/six Harriers. V/STOL carrier mode: 20 Harriers/four Seahawk LAMPS-III helicopters.
Armament: Two eight-tube Mk 29 launchers for Sea Sparrow/three Mk 15 Phalanx CIWS

Tarawa Class Amphibious Assault Ships

The five ships of the *Tarawa* class, built in the 1970s, are currently the largest amphibious ships afloat, displacing more even than the Soviet *Kiev* class V/STOL carriers. They differ from the newer *Wasps* primarily in that they were not designed with the LCAC landing craft in mind and can accommodate only one, though they can handle the equivalent of four LCUs in their docking wells and can, in addition, stow two LCMs and two LCPs elsewhere. They provide 33,720 sq ft of vehicle parking space, 117,000 cu ft of dry cargo space and can carry about 2000 troops. Their nominal air complement for amphibious assault missions is the equivalent of 38 Sea

LHA 4 Nassau (Tarawa *class*).

Knight helicopters, but they have been observed carrying up to 19 Harriers, as well as heavy lift helicopters, so it must be assumed that, like the *Wasps*, they can also be used in a V/STOL carrier mode.

They are the only amphibious ships to carry five-inch guns – three single-mount Mk 22. These can be used for AA but are primarily intended for shore bombardment. All ships except *Saipan* (which has one) currently have two eight-tube Sea Sparrow launchers, and all are due to be fitted with two Phalanx mounts in the near future, at which time one of the mounts of the Mk 22 five-inch guns will be removed. Their radar suites are relatively up-to-date and doubtless will be up-graded in the course of regular overhauls. As of 1987 *Tarawa*, *Belleau Wood* and *Peleliu* were assigned to the Pacific, and *Saipan* and *Nassau* to the Atlantic.

Names: LHA 1 *Tarawa*, LHA 2 *Saipan*, LHA 3 *Belleau Wood*, LHA 4 *Nassau*, LHA 5 *Peleliu*
Displacement: 39,300 tons fully loaded
Length: 778 ft
Propulsion: Two steam turbines delivering a total of 70,000 shp
Speed: 24 kt
Combat load: 2000 troops/equivalent of four LCU, two LCM and two LCP (only one LCAC)/equivalent of 38 CH-46 helicopters or 19 Harriers and four Sea Knights.
Armament: Two (except LHA 2) eight-tube Mk 25 Sea Sparrow launchers/three Mk 22 single-mount 5-inch/54-cal guns/six Mk 67 20 mm guns/one (LHA 2,4) Mk 15 Phalanx CIWS (all units to receive two Mk 15 mounts at the expense of one Mk 22 mount)

RIGHT: *LPH 9* Guam (Iwo Jima *class*).
FAR RIGHT: *An AV-8A Harrier of Marine Fighter Squadron 231.*
BELOW: *LPH 10* Tripoli (Iwo Jima *class*).

Iwo Jima Class Amphibious Assault Ships

The seven ships of the *Iwo Jima* class, built in the 1960s, were the world's first carrier-like helicopter assault ships. Much smaller than the *Wasps* or *Tarawas*, they cannot carry landing craft other than two small LCVPs on davits. As a class the *Iwo Jimas* will be approaching block obsolescence in the mid-1990s. The Navy had originally counted on all 11-ship *Wasp* class as their replacements, but now that it seems that only five *Wasps* may be built, the aerial capabilities of the amphibious assault ship fleet of the late 1990s may be somewhat less than had been hoped.

Typically the *Iwo Jimas* carry 20-24 Sea Knight, four Sea Stallion and four utility or attack helicopters, but they have also been known to carry aircraft complements composed largely of Harriers or the RH-53 minesweeper variant of the Sea Stallion. All are armed with two eight-tube Sea Sparrow launchers and two Phalanx mounts, as well as four twin-mounted Mk 22 three-inch dual-purpose guns. They have a cruising range of about 10,000 nm. *Okinawa*, *Tripoli* and *New Orleans* operate in the Pacific; the others in the Atlantic.

Names: LPH 2 *Iwo Jima*, LPH 3 *Okinawa*, LPH 7 *Guadalcanal*, LPH 9 *Guam*, LPH 10 *Tripoli*, LPH 11 *New Orleans*, LPH 12 *Inchon*
Displacement: 19,300 tons full load
Length: 556 ft
Propulsion: One steam turbine delivering 23,000 shp
Speed: 22 kt
Combat load: Typically 20-24 CH-46/four CH-53/four UH-1 or four AH-1 helicopters
Armament: Two eight-tube Mk 25 Sea Sparrow launchers/ four twin-mounted Mk 22 3-inch/50-cal guns/ two Mk 15 Phalanx CIWS

Whidbey Island Dock Landing Ships

Though they may carry a few helicopters, dock landing ships are primarily intended to deploy landing craft (*ie*, just the reverse of the *Iwo Jimas*). The newest ships in this category, the *Whidbey Islands*, were specifically designed to accommodate air-cushion LCACs, four of which can be contained in the ships' docking wells. Alternatively, the wells can hold three LCUs, 21 LCMs or 64 LVTP amphibious assault vehicles. In addition, one LCM, two LCPLs and one LCVP can be carried on deck. Each ship can transport over 500 armed troops and provides about 5260 cu ft of space for palletized cargo. The *Whidbey Islands* have a range of about 8000 nm.

The ships have no hangars but can carry two Sea Stallion helicopters on open platforms. AA defense is based on two Phalanx mounts, supplemented by two 25 mm Mk 88 Bushmaster or two 20-mm Mk 16 guns.

Present plans call for eight ships of this class to be built. Three were in service by mid-1987, and the eighth unit is expected to join the fleet sometime in 1990. As a class, the *Whidbey Islands* are intended to replace the eight-ship *Thomaston* class, most of which are already in reserve.

A new six-ship class of cargo-carrying variants of the *Whidbey Islands* – so far known only as the LSD 49 class – has been proposed for the 1990s. They would carry the equivalent of only two LCACs in their docking wells in exchange for much expanded cargo space, but would otherwise be gener-

ally similar to the *Whidbey Islands*. Whether these ships will in fact be built remains to be seen.

Names: LSD 41 *Whidbey Island*, LSD 42 *Germantown*, LSD 43 *Fort McHenry*, plus two building and three planned.
Displacement: 15,814 tons fully loaded
Length: 580 ft
Propulsion: Four diesels delivering a total of 41,600 hp (34,000 hp sustained)
Speed: 22 kt
Combat load: 500+ troops/three LCAC or three LCU and one LCM or 22 LCM or 64 LVTP/two CH-53 helicopters
Armament Two 25 mm Mk 88 Bushmaster or two 20 mm Mk 16 guns/two Mk 15 Phalanx CIWS

An artist's rendering of LSD 41 Whidbey Island, *leader of the Navy's newest class of dock landing ships.*

Anchorage Class Dock Landing Ships

The five *Anchorage* class ships were built in the late 1960s and early 1970s, before the advent of the LCAC. Yet fortuitously, because of their large docking wells, they can handle up to four of these large air-cushion craft. The intended accommodation, however, was for three LCUs or eight-15 LCMs. Their total vehicle storage space measures about 15,800 sq ft. They can carry a total of up to 375 troops.

They may or may not carry up to two helicopters, since the helicopter deck is removable. Their present somewhat outdated AA armament of six three-inch Mk 22 guns in twin mounts is being supplemented by two Phalanx mounts (presumably at the expense of at least one set of Mk 22s).

It is unclear how long these ships can be retained in active service, since the youngest was laid down in 1970 and no Service Life Extension Programs have been planned for the class. At present *Portland* and *Pensacola* serve in the Pacific, and the other three in the Atlantic.

Names: LSD 36 *Anchorage*, LSD 37 *Portland*, LSD 38 *Pensacola*, LSD 39 *Mount Vernon*, LSD 40 *Fort Fisher*
Displacement: 13,700 tons fully loaded
Length: 534 ft
Propulsion: Two steam turbines delivering a total of 24,000 shp
Speed: 20 kt
Combat load: Up to 375 troops/three LCAC or three LCU plus eight-15 LCM or 50 LVT/up to two CH-53 helicopters
Armament: Six 3-inch/50 cal twin-mounted Mk 22 guns/two Mk 15 Phalanx CIWS to be added

Thomaston Class Dock Landing Ships

The eight ships of the *Thomaston* class are the Navy's oldest dock landing ships, all having been built in the 1950s. Most have already been retired, and none will remain on active

ABOVE: *LPD 8* Dubuque (Austin *class*).
ABOVE RIGHT: *LPD 4 Austin*, the class leader.
LEFT ABOVE: *LSD 40* Fort Fisher (Anchorage *class*).
LEFT BELOW: *LSD 32* Spiegel Grove (Thomaston *class*).

duty by the end of the 1980s. Despite their age they have, like the *Anchorage* class ships, capacious docking wells and can accommodate up to three of the new air-cushion LCACs (or three LCUs or nine-18 LCMs, depending on their size). They could, therefore, be more than usually valuable additions to the National Defense Reserve Fleet.
Names: LSD 28 *Thomaston*, LSD 29 *Plymouth Rock*, LSD 30 *Fort Snelling*, LSD 31 *Point Defiance*, LSD 32 *Spiegel Grove*, LSD 33 *Alamo*, LSD 34 *Hermitage*, LSD 35 *Monticello*
Displacement: 11,270 tons fully loaded
Length: 510 ft
Propulsion: Two steam turbines delivering a total of 24,000 shp
Speed: 22 kt
Combat load: Up to 320 troops/three LCAC or three LCU or up to 18 LCM/up to two CH-53 helicopters
Armament: Six 3-inch/50-cal Mk 22 guns in three twin mounts (LSD 34 also two Mk 15 Phalanx CIWS)

Austin Class Amphibious Transport Docks

Amphibious transport docks are similar to dock landing ships in that they transport troop and landing craft but have little aerial capacity of their own. (Though, like LSDs, they can receive transient helicopters from amphibious assault ships.) They differ from LSDs primarily in having smaller docking

wells and more space for berthing troops and parking vehicles. Fortunately, the docking wells are not so small that they cannot be modified to accommodate up to two of the new air-cushion LCACs. All 11 ships of the *Austin* class are scheduled for Service Life Extension Programs in the late 1980s.

The *Austin* ships can carry up to 930 troops and provide about 15,700 sq ft of vehicle storage space. As an alternative to LCACs, their docking wells can accommodate one LCU and three LCMs or up to nine LCMs, depending on size. At least two more LCMs can be carried on the helicopter deck. They can also accommodate up to six Sea Knight helicopters, but only on a temporary basis. Their older AA armament of four three-inch Mk 22 guns in two twin mounts is currently being supplemented with the addition of two Phalanx mounts. The *Austins* have a range of about 7700 nm. LPDs 5-12 serve in the Pacific; the remainder in the Atlantic.
Names: LPD 4 *Austin*, LPD 5 *Ogden*, LPD 6 *Duluth*, LPD 7 *Cleveland*, LPD 8 *Dubuque*, LPD 9 *Denver*, LPD 10 *Juneau*, LPD 12 *Shreveport*, LPD 13 *Nashville*, LPD 14 *Trenton*, LPD 15 *Ponce*
Displacement: 16,900 tons fully loaded
Length: 569 ft
Propulsion: Two steam turbines delivering 24,000 shp
Speed: 20 kt
Combat load: Up to 930 troops/two LCAC or one LCU and five LCM or up to 11 LCM or 28 LVT/up to six CH-46 helicopters (temporarily)
Armament: Four 3-inch/50-cal Mk 22 guns in twin mounts/ also being fitted with two Mk 15 Phalanx CIWS

The amphibious transport, dock, LPD 2 Vancouver *(Raleigh class).*

Raleigh Class Amphibious Transport Docks

The two ships of the *Raleigh* class are basically similar to the *Austins* – were, in a sense, prototypes for them. Although the *Raleighs'* docking wells are slightly shorter, they can still be modified to handle two LCACs (or one LCU and three or four LCMs). Unlike the *Austins*, the *Raleighs*, which were built in the early 1960s, will not receive SLEP modernization, though they will receive such improvements in regular overhauls as the addition of two Phalanx mounts for AA defense. How long into the 1990s the *Raleighs* will continue in active service is moot.

Names: LPD 1 *Raleigh*, LPD 2 *Vancouver*
Displacement: 14,650 tons fully loaded
Length: 522 ft
Propulsion: Two steam turbines delivering 24,000 shp
Speed: 21 kt
Combat load: Up to 930 troops/two LCAC or one LCU and up to six LCM or 24 LVT/up to six CH-46 helicopters
Armament: Six 3-inch/50-cal Mk 22 guns in twin mounts/to be fitted with two Mk 15 Phalanx CIWS (possibly at the expense of one Mk 22 mount)

Newport Class Tank Landing Ships

In conception these tank landing ships built in the late 1960s and early 1970s pre-date the current predilection for over-the-horizon amphibious capabilities. Like their World War II ancestors they were meant to unload directly onto hostile beaches or onto pontoon causeways built out from the beaches, but unlike their progenitors they are ships of considerable sophistication.

Their 20-kt sustained speed enables them to keep up with fast-moving modern amphibious squadrons – something the ponderous earlier LSTs could not have done. They can carry some 500 tons of cargo and 430 troops on about 19,000 sq ft of deck space. Their 112-ft bow ramps are lowered by two fixed derrick arms and can support 75 tons of men and equipment. A second ramp in the stern can unload amphibious vehicles into the water. They are fitted with side-thrust propellers to help them 'mate' with causeways, and they can themselves carry up to four sections of causeway lashed to their sides. Their AA armament of four three-inch Mk 22 guns in two twin mounts is being supplemented (or possibly replaced) by two Phalanx gatling gun mounts. Of the 20 ships in the original class two have been placed in reserve and the remaining 18 are evenly divided between the Atlantic and Pacific.

Names: LST 1179 *Newport*, LST 1180 *Manitowoc*, LST 1181 *Sumpter*, LST 1182 *Fresno*, LST 1183 *Peoria*, LST 1184 *Frederick,* LST 1185 *Tuscaloosa*, LST 1188 *Saginaw*, LST 1189 *San Bernardino*, LST 1190 *Boulder**, LST 1191 *Racine**, LST 1192 *Spartanburg County*, LST 1193 *Fairfax County*, LST 1194 *La Moure County*, LST 1995 *Barbour County*, LST 1196 *Harlan County,* LST 1197 *Barnstable County*, LST 1198 *Bristol County*
Displacement: 8342 tons fully loaded
Length: 522 ft
Propulsion: Six diesels delivering a total of 16,500 shp
Speed: 22 kt
Combat load: 430 troops/four LCVP (davits)/500 tons of cargo/platform for one helicopter

Armament: Four 3-inch/50-cal Mk 22 guns in two twin mounts/being fitted with two Mk 15 Phalanx CIWS
*In reserve

Reserve Tank Landing Ships

Three LSTs of the 8000-ton *De Soto County* class and six LSTs of the 5800-ton *Terrebonne County* class are in reserve. The *De Sotos* can carry up to 575 troops or 23 medium tanks. The *Terrebonnes* can carry up to 400 troops or 17 LVTs. Both are of conventional bow-doors-and-ramp design.

Charleston Class Amphibious Cargo Ships

Amphibious cargo ships differ from other cargo ships in that they are built for relatively high speed and are designed to unload equipment and supplies rapidly onto helicopters and landing craft. The five *Charleston* class ships were the first to be built specifically to fulfill this role. They can carry up to 225 troops and have some 38,000 sq ft of vehicle storage space. In addition they can carry up to nine LCMs and two LCVPs. They are scheduled to receive two Phalanx mounts to supplement their present AA defense of six three-inch Mk 22 guns in three twin mounts.

Some of the *Charlestons* had been placed in reserve, but all were reactivated in the early 1980s.

Names: LKA 113 *Charleston*, LKA 114 *Durham*, LKA 115 *Mobile*, LKA 116 *St Louis*, LKA 117 *El Paso*
Displacement: 20,700 tons fully loaded
Length: 576 ft
Propulsion: One steam turbine delivering 22,000 shp
Speed: 20+ kt
Combat load: 225 troops/nine LCM and two LCVP
Armament: Six 3-inch/50-cal Mk 22 guns in three twin mounts/being fitted with two Mk 15 Phalanx CIWS

ABOVE: *The bow ramp of a Newport class tank landing ship.*

BELOW: *The amphibious command ship LCC 19 Blue Ridge.*

Command Ships

There are four other ships that might be added to the active amphibious force in time of need. Two 19,200-ton highly sophisticated command ships of the *Blue Ridge* class were originally earmarked for the amphibious force but since 1970 have served as flagships for the Second and Seventh Fleets. Conceivably there might be circumstances in which they might be reverted to an amphibious role. These ships are fitted with highly modern radar suites and satellite communications, as well as an Amphibious Command Information System and a Naval Intelligence Processing System.

Names: LCC 19 *Blue Ridge*, LCC 20 *Mount Whitney*
Displacement: 19,290 tons full load
Length: 620 ft
Propulsion: 1 steam turbiine delivering 22,000 shp
Speed: 21.5 kt
Combat load: 150 troops/three LCP and two LCVP/helicopter platform
Armament: Two eight-tube Mk 25 Sea Sparrow launchers/four 3- inch/50-cal Mk 22 guns in two twin mounts/*Blue Ridge* one Mk 15 Phalanx CIWS

Two other amphibious ships have been diverted to the flagship/command ship role, the *Austin* class *Coronado* (now designated AGF 11) and the *Raleigh* class *La Salle* (now AGF 3).

LCAC Type Air-cushion Landing Craft

The revolutionary new LCAC air-cushion landing craft began to join the fleet late in 1984. Teething troubles with the propulsion system caused procurement to be interrupted after the first 33 units were delivered, but most of the problems now appear to have been solved and production is expected to resume in 1988. Unloaded, the 88-ton LCAC can skim above the surface of the water at 50 kt, and even when fully loaded and weighing around 200 tons, the LCAC's speed is still about 40 kt. Its range is 200 nm, and its 4600-cu ft of cargo space can accommodate 250 fully equipped troops or up to 75 tons of cargo, including, for example, three LVTs or one 48-ton M60 tank, plus a smaller vehicle. Since it can skim over four-foot-high obstacles, shoals and low reefs cannot deter it, and it therefore has access to an estimated 70 percent of the world's beaches. It has a 29-ft-wide bow ramp and a 15-ft-wide stern ramp. It is propelled by two large shrouded air-screws mounted on the stern superstructure. It usually carries no armament but is equipped with navigational radar.

ABOVE: *An LCM(8) landing craft.* BELOW: *An artist's rendering of the new LCAC air-cushion landing craft coming on shore.*

LCU 1610 Type Utility Landing Craft

The LCUs are the largest conventional landing craft now in US service. Between 1960 and 1976 over 50 of the LCU 1610 type were built, but since several units have been stricken, transferred to other navies or reclassified, the number now in active service with the Navy is about 40. They are 135 ft long and when fully loaded displace 390 tons. They can carry 350 troops or 190 tons of cargo (including up to two M60 tanks). They are fitted with a large bow ramp and a smaller stern ramp. Not normally armed, they have a maximum speed of 11 kt and a maximum range of 1200 nm.

LCM(8) Mod 1 and Mod 2 Type Mechanized Landing Craft

The Navy has over 200 of these medium-sized landing craft on active duty or in reserve. The welded-steel-hull Mod 1 type is the heavier of the two. Seventy-four ft long, it displaces 130 tons fully loaded. It can carry up to 200 troops or 60 tons of

ABOVE: *Troops come on shore from an LCM(6) landing craft.*
BELOW: *A Marine LVTP-7 amphibious personnel carrier.*

cargo (including one M60 tank). Its maximum speed is nine kt, and its range 140 nm. The aluminum-hull Mod 2 type displaces 107 tons fully loaded but can carry about the same load as the Mod 1 at 12 kt over a slightly longer range. Both craft have bow ramps only, and neither normally carries any armament.

LCM(6) Mod 2 Type Mechanized Landing Craft

The Navy has well over 100 of these welded-steel craft, and they continue to be built. They are 56 ft long and displace 62 tons fully loaded. They can carry 120 troops or 34 tons of cargo. Their speed is 10 kt, and their maximum range is 130 nm. They have a single bow ramp and are not normally armed.

LCVP Type Vehicle and Personnel Landing Craft

The Navy has over 135 of these small landing craft, whose hulls are constructed of glass-reinforced plastic. They are 36 ft long and displace 14 tons when fully loaded. They can carry 36 troops or a cargo of nearly four tons. Their speed is nine kt, and their range about 110 nm. They unload from a single bow ramp.

LVT Type Tracked Landing Vehicles

The Marines currently operate nearly 1000 amphibious tracked landing vehicles of the LVT-7 series. The most important variant is the LVTP-7 personnel carrier. (The other variants are the LVTC-7 command and control vehicle and the LVTR-7 recovery vehicle.) The LVTP-7 weighs 50,350 lbs fully loaded. It can carry 25 troops or 10,000 lbs of cargo at eight kt in the water and 20-30 mph on land, and it can operate in surf up to 10 feet high. Its range in the water is over 50 nm, and its range on land is about 300 mi. It is normally armed with one 50-cal machine gun in a 360-degree revolving turret, but it has been test-fitted with a 40-mm cannon.

Chapter 11
PATROL
SHIPS AND
CRAFT

Originally projected as a class of 30, the Pegasus *class missile patrol boats proved so expensive that Navy interest waned and only six were built.*

ABOVE: *This stern view of PHM 2* Hercules *shows the boat's unique waterjet propulsion system.*
RIGHT: *PHM 1* Pegasus, *the class leader.*

PGG) built in US shipyards were shipped to Saudi Arabia. Other types of small craft were sent to other foreign navies. In fact, the Navy now relies fairly heavily on friendly foreign navies to make up its deficiencies in this type of combatant.

Many of the special warfare and inshore craft are assigned to Naval Reserve Forces. The hydrofoil missile craft (PHM) constitute Patrol Combat Missile Hydrofoil Squadron 2, based at the Naval Air Station in Key West, Florida. Other small craft units are based in San Diego and Norfolk.

The latter take part in coastal operations. Their mission is to provide a coastal and inshore warfare capability such as gunfire and spotter support and delivery and recovery of special combat teams called SEALs (Sea, Air, Land Teams).

The smaller patrol boats and craft are not named. They are designated according to their hull length and type and when they were made. The designation 65PB776, for example, indicates that the boat was the sixth 65-ft PB-type craft built in 1977.

Pegasus Class Hydrofoil Missile Patrol Boats

The difficulties and delays experienced in the building of this series of heavily armed, high speed missile craft were indicative of the Navy's attitude toward small patrol craft. The design was proposed by Admiral Zumwalt, Chief of Naval Operations from 1970 to 1974. At least 30 vessels were included in the original plan. When Zumwalt retired, the program was reduced to only the prototype. But Congress had already funded six boats and insisted on their completion. Work started on the second boat in the series, PHM 2 *Hercules*, in 1974. Work was halted a year later because of cost increases in PHM 1 *Pegasus*. She was reauthorized, and work started again in 1980.

The hydrofoils of the *Pegasus* boats are fully submerged during hydrofoil operation. Approximately 32 percent of the dynamic lift is provided by the single bow foil and about 68 percent by the double-strut after foil. Control and lift augmentation is provided by flaps fitted to the trailing edges of the bow and after foils. The foils retract when the craft is operating in its hullborne mode.

Historically, the Navy has shown little peacetime interest in small combatant craft. Part of the reason for this is that the Navy's primary strategic mission calls for long-distance, blue water operations. Also, it was generally felt in the past that small craft for coastal and riverine operations could be quickly developed. The flaw in this policy became apparent during the Vietnam War, when the Navy had to buy Norwegian-built small craft and adapt commercial designs for the coastal and riverine operations that were so much a part of that conflict.

In the years following the Vietnam War the Navy has made efforts to remain current in small craft design and tactics. By the mid 1980s, six hydrofoil missile craft and a fairly large number of inshore and special warfare craft were in service. Old attitudes die hard, however. The six extant hydrofoil craft are the remains of an ambitious program of at least 30 vessels proposed by Chief of Naval Operations Admiral Zumwalt in the 1970s, and considerable Congressional pressure was required to get these six units built after Zumwalt's retirement.

From 1980 to 1982 a series of small missile craft (PCG/

The *Pegasus* class boats have waterjet propulsion. Foilborne propulsion is provided by a single waterjet driven by an LM 2500 gas turbine via reduction gears. The propulsor, mounted on the foil, can pump 141,000 gallons of water a minute. Speeds in excess of 50 kt are possible even in eight- to 13-ft seas. Hullborne propulsion is provided by two V-8 diesel engines powering twin water jets capable of pumping 30,000 gallons of water a minute.

Originally intended to be armed with two single Harpoon launching tubes, the design has changed to accommodate two non-reloadable quad canisters mounted aft.

Names: PHM 1 *Pegasus*, PHM 2 *Hercules*, PHM 3 *Taurus*, PHM 4 *Aquila*, PHM 5 *Aries*, PHM 5 *Gemini*
Displacement: 242 tons full load
Length: 147 ft (foils retracted)
Propulsion: Two diesels of 1636 shp and two waterjets when hullborne/two gas turbines of 16,000-19,416 shp and two waterjets when foilborne
Speed: 12 kt hullborne/50+ foilborne
Armament: Eight Harpoon/one 76-mm Mk 75 AA gun

Special Warfare Craft, Medium

This new class of air-cushion small combatants is expected to begin joining the fleet in the late 1980s. They were at first to be classed as Multimission Patrol Boats (PBMs), but this has been changed to Special Warfare Craft, Medium (SWCM), and it is now thought that they will be used primarily in conjunction with amphibious operations (*ie*, will be carried in the docking wells of amphibious ships). So far, 18 are planned, nine for each coast.

Unlike the LCAC air-cushion landing craft, the SWCMs can carry only about 16 armed troops, and these presumably will be SEAL special forces teams. The SWCMs displace about 115 tons full and can travel at about 35 kt. Plans call for them to be armed with two 25-mm Bushmaster chain guns or 25-mm Sea Vulcan gatlings, as well as hand-held Stinger SAMs and two machine guns. Some sources say the class name will be *Viking*.

A patrol boat of the PB Mk III 'Sea Spectre' class.

Designation: SWCM
Displacement: 83 tons light/115 tons full load
Length: 78 ft
Propulsion: 2 diesels (two shafts) delivering 3600 shp/two diesel lift fan engines (six fans) delivering 680 hp
Speed: *c* 35 kt
Armament: Two 25-mm Sea Vulcan gatling or 25-mm Mk 88 Bushmaster/Stinger/mg

PB Mk III and Mk IV 'Sea Spectre' Class Patrol Craft

The Mk III is a modification of commercial craft used to support offshore drilling rigs. It was developed for the US and foreign navies as a multi-mission inshore warfare craft. Its low profile and quiet engines make it especially suitable for clandestine operations. Its armament is variable and surprisingly heavy. At one time it was used for tests of the Penguin Mk 2 ASW missile. Seventeen of the all-aluminum Mk IIIs are in service. Three more such craft, with hulls lengthened 3 ft, designated Mk IVs, entered service in 1985.

Designation: PB Mk III 'Sea Spectre'/PB Mk IV 'Sea Spectre'
Length: 65 ft/68 ft
Propulsion: Three diesels (three shafts) delivering 1950 shp
Speed: 30 kt
Armament: One 40-mm Mk 3 AA gun or two 25-mm Sea Vulcan gatlings or two 25-mm Mk 88 Bushmaster chain guns/ one 81-mm mortar/mg

SCWL 'Seafox' Class Special Warfare Craft, Light

Like the SWCMs, the 'Seafox' SWCLs are intended mainly to be used by SEAL special forces teams, often in conjunction with amphibious operations. These small three-man boats are of glass-reinforced plastic construction and can travel over 30 kt. They have been in service since 1981, and the Navy now has 70 of them in its inventory.

Designation: SWCL 'Seafox'
Displacement: 12 tons full load
Length: 36 ft

Propulsion: Two diesels (two shafts) delivering 900 shp
Speed: 30+ kt
Armament: Four stations for mg

Other Patrol Craft

The Navy still has two PB Mk 1 class patrol boats in service. These 27-ton boats lost out to the Mk IIIs in service-evaluation competition.

Of the 125 PCF 'Swift' class Patrol Craft, Fast, built for operations in Vietnam, only two remain in service, and two are in the Naval reserve. These are six-man 17-tonners armed with machine guns and a mortar.

Of the more than 500 PBR Patrol Boats, Riverine, built during the Vietnam period, 32 remain, all in the Naval Reserve. These nine-ton five-man boats have fibreglass hulls and pump-jet propulsion to facilitate maneuver in shallow, debris-filled waters. They carry machine guns and mortars.

Similarly, of the 25 PTF Fast Patrol Boats acquired during the Vietnam War, three remain in reserve. These relatively large (112 tons full load) craft can be configured for minelaying and ASW as well as patrol. They can be armed with mortars and 40- and 20-mm AA guns.

ABOVE: *Much of the early testing of missile-launching hydrofoils was done with the experimental craft PCH 1 High Point.*

ABOVE LEFT: *A fast patrol boat, PTF class, now in reserve.*

Chapter 12
MINE COUNTER-MEASURES SHIPS AND CRAFT

Until the Avenger *class ships began entering the fleet in 1986, the only oceangoing minesweepers in the Navy were the MSOs of the 1950s. Here, MSO 455* Implicit.

Until the 1980s no aspect of naval combat had been more neglected by the United States than mine warfare. In the more than quarter-century between the end of World War II and 1980 the Navy had introduced only one significant mine countermeasure innovation – the force of 30 Navy and 16 Marine RH-53D minesweeping helicopters (the total now reduced by seven, thanks to losses suffered in the failed mission to rescue the Teheran hostages in 1980). By the same token, the Navy's efforts to develop new types of mines had been fitful and somewhat disappointing, and as for minelaying, that function had been (and still is) entirely removed from surface ships and confined to aircraft and submarines.

This is all the more surprising in view of the role that mine warfare played in World War II. More ships were sunk by mines in that conflict than by any other agency – 1.4 million tons of Allied merchant shipping alone. It is still widely believed that even without either the dropping of the atomic bomb or an invasion of the home islands Japan would probably have been obliged to surrender by 1946 as the result of the gigantic US mine blockade (Operation Starvation) that had sealed off all her ports and annihilated her merchant marine.

Certainly the Soviet Union has followed a very different course than that of the United States in respect to mine warfare. The Soviets have built up immense stockpiles of mines of all sorts since 1945, and if their current mine technology is still not quite as advanced as it is in the West, it is certainly not so far behind as to make much difference. Soviet minelaying capacity is impressive. Over 585 aircraft and 265 helicopters are fitted to lay mines, as are more than 600 ships, fully a third of them major surface combatants. For minesweeping the Soviet Navy maintains more than 300 specialist ships in its inventory (though, to be sure, only a handful are of the most advanced type).

In 1981 the Reagan Administration initiated a belated program to rebuild the Navy's mine countermeasures capabilities. At that time the Navy's entire surface minesweeper force consisted of 21 Korean War-vintage ocean-going ships and seven tugboat-sized inshore craft. Although the ships had been retrofitted with SQQ-14 sonars and improved communications gear in the 1970s, they were still far from able to cope with all the advances in mine technology that had

LEFT: *An RH-53E Sea Stallion towing a minesweeping sled. Sweeping by helicopter was one of the Navy's few innovations in this neglected field.*
FAR LEFT: *A head-on view of MSO 489* Gallant *(Aggressive class).*

occurred since they were launched. The old-fashioned mechanical methods of sweeping now had to be supplemented with increasingly sophisticated magnetic and acoustical sweeps, and a whole new technique called 'minehunting' had been developed to deal with the new generation of mobile sea-bottom mines that are largely resistant to sweeping of any kind.

In minehunting the exact location of a mine must first be established through the use of computerized sonars and navigational equipment of the highest order. Then the mine must be classified as to type. And finally it must be disposed of by a method appropriate to that type. The most advanced disposal system is one that is centered on small remote-controlled robot submarines that can identify mines via various onboard sensors (including closed-circuit TV link with the mother ship) and can then be instructed to cut cables, lay nearby explosive charges or take other appropriate action.

The Reagan initiative has so far resulted in one new class of mine countermeasures ships, the *Avenger* class MCMs, that have already begun to join the fleet, and a second, the *Cardinal* class MSHs, that are due to begin entering service

in 1988. A third class, tentatively designated CMH, is under consideration. The robot submarine developed for use by such ships, called the SLQ-48 MNS (Mine Neutralization System), is 12 ft long, weighs 2200 lb, can travel at 6 kt and is fitted with rear and side thrusters, TV cameras, sonar, an acoustic responder, cable cutters, destructor charges and so on. The ships themselves are equipped with ultra-sensitive SQQ-30 or -32 variable-depth sonars, Precision Integrated Navigation Systems (PINS), and other state-of-the-art MCM features, and their hulls and propulsion systems are specially designed to present the lowest possible signatures to influence-type mines.

A peculiarity of the US MCM ships is that they are all, with the exception of four elderly MSOs that are used for test purposes, operated by the Naval Reserve Force. They are, however, maintained in a very high state of readiness and could be reactivated on short notice.

Welcome as the revived US interest in MCM is, it is late in coming and will be slow to show significant material results. Fortunately, several of America's NATO allies, as well as Japan, maintain and are rapidly up-grading capable MCM forces of their own.

*An artist's impression of MSH 1
Cardinal, leader of a class of
coastal minehunters due to begin
joining the fleet in 1988.*

Cardinal Class Minehunters

The *Cardinals*, due to begin joining the fleet in 1988, will be the only air-cushion vessels in the Navy apart from the amphibious LCACs and special warfare SWCMs. Their semi-catamaran-type hulls will be made of a glass-reinforced plastic foam that will help to reduce their underwater magnetic and acoustic signatures. They will normally operate fairly close inshore and will not be equipped for sweeping influence mines. They will, however, carry one deep-diving SLQ-48 MNS robot submersible and will be fitted from the outset with SQQ-32 variable depth sonar. The Navy plans to purchase 17, all of which will be operated by the Naval Reserve Force.

Names: MSH 1 *Cardinal*, and 16 others
Displacement: 440 tons
Length: 189 ft
Propulsion: Two diesels (two shafts) delivering 1160 shp/two diesels for the lift fans delivering 1650 hp
Speed: *c* 15 kt
Armament: Two mg

Avenger Class Minesweeper/ Minehunters

When the *Avengers* began to join the fleet in 1986 they were the Navy's first new MCM ships in nearly 30 years. Not unnaturally, they bore little resemblance to their predecessors of 1958. Their wooden hulls are sheathed in sandwiched plastic foam and their superstructures are made of fibreglass. They can sweep magnetic and acoustic mines, as well as (mechanically) mines moored up to depths of 600 ft, and they carry two SLQ-48 MNS robot submersibles for deep-water mine-hunting and neutralization. The first five of the class will be equipped with SQQ-30 variable-depth sonar but will be back-fitted with the longer-range SQQ-32 after it becomes available. Information from the submersible, the sonar and the SSN-2(V) Precision Integrated Navigation System is fed into a fully automated mine countermeasures information center that can review, plot and evaluate mine information. So far, 14 ships of the class have been planned. All will be placed in the Naval Reserve Force.

Names: MCM 1 *Avenger*, MCM 2 *Defender*, MCM 3 *Sentry*, MCM 4 *Champion*, MCM 5 *Guardian*, nine more planned.
Displacement: 1312 tons full load
Length: 224 ft
Propulsion: Four diesels geared to two shafts and delivering up to 2280 shp/one 350-hp Omnithruster
Speed: 16 kt
Armament: Two mg (Mk 15 Phalanx may be installed)

Acme and Aggressive Class Ocean Minesweepers

These elderly minesweepers are essentially similar in design, the two *Acmes* (MSO 509 *Adroit* and MSO 511 *Affray*)

MSO 448 Illusive (Aggressive class).

being a foot longer than the *Aggressives* and displacing 30 more tons when fully loaded. All are wooden-hulled and are fitted with non-magnetic bronze and stainless-steel machinery. They carry SQQ-14 variable depth sonars and SPS-53 radars (due to be replaced with SPS-64 on the *Aggressives*). All are in the NRF. Names apart, the specifications below refer to the *Aggressives*.

Names: *Acme* Class: MSO 509 *Adroit* and MSO 511 *Affray*. *Aggressive* Class: MSO 427 *Constant*, MSO 433 *Engage*, MSO 437 *Enhance*, MSO 438 *Esteem*, MSO 439 *Excel*, MSO 440 *Exploit*, MSO 441 *Exultant*, MSO 442 *Fearless*, MSO 443 *Fidelity*, MSO 446 *Fortify*, MSO 448 *Illusive*, MSO 449 *Impervious*, MSO 455 *Implicit*, MSO 456 *Inflict*, MSO 464 *Pluck*, MSO 488 *Conquest*, MSO 489 *Gallant*, MSO 490 *Leader*, MSO 492 *Pledge*
Displacement: 750 tons full load
Length: 172 ft
Propulsion: Two diesels (two shafts) delivering 2400 shp
Speed: 14 kt
Armament: Two mg

Minesweeping Boats

The Navy's fleet of minesweeping boats at present consists primarily of a single unit of the 80-ton MSB 29 class and six units of the 30-ton MSB 5 class. Recently the Navy initiated a 'Craft of Opportunity Program' (COOP) in which various odds and ends of boats, such as those used for training at the Naval Academy and the Officer Candidate School, or commercial fishing craft, could be converted for MCM duties. The plan calls for 22 such craft to be operated by the Navy in peacetime, with 66 more civilian craft being earmarked for rapid conversion in case of emergency.

The CMH Proposal

The Marinette Marine Company of Wisconsin has proposed a new class of coastal minehunters, tentatively designated CMH, that would not only require less than a third of the crew needed for the *Avengers* but, because of their high automation, would be simpler to operate.

Chapter 13 SUPPORT SHIPS

Typical of the many types and classes of support ships in the Navy is the replenishment oiler T-AO 143 Neosho, *operated by the Military Sealift Command.*

LEFT: *The fleet tug T-ATF 166* Powatan.
FAR LEFT: *The replenishment oiler T-AO 105* Mispillon, *class leader.*

LEFT: *The* Cimmeron *class oiler AO 178* Monongahela.
FAR LEFT: *The replenishment oiler AOR 4* Savannah (Wichita *class*).

The term 'support ship' is used here to refer to any of a large number of nominally noncombatant vessels used in some capacity to supply or support Navy and Marine combat forces. (In formal Navy parlance, it should be noted, the term 'support ship' has a more restricted meaning). Indeed, there are so many varieties of support ships that in this chapter it will be possible to describe only the most important and/or representative types.

Support ships fall into three main administrative groups: those that are on active duty and under direct Navy control, those that are on active duty and under the control of the civilian-manned Military Sealift Command and those that are in the Ready Reserve Force of the National Defense Reserve Fleet.

The support ships in service and under direct Navy control are generally referred to as auxiliaries, and their designations usually begin with the letter 'A.' They include a number of specialist types, such as tenders, oilers, ammunition carriers and repair ships, that are capable of servicing fleet units while they are under way or of giving direct support to Marine and Naval forces when they are far from their home bases. Also included in the auxiliary category are a miscellany of smaller service vessels, and experimental and training ships.

Some of the ships in the Military Sealift Command are similar in type to auxiliaries, but they are considered by the Navy to be non-commissioned and are manned by civilian civil servants or contract personnel, even though the MSC is headed by an active-duty Navy flag officer. Some MSC ships are owned outright by the Navy, while others are under long-term charter. Although the MSC operates a wide variety of types, the emphasis is on cargo-carriers, oilers and transports. Among the many MSC-operated ships are those of the Maritime Prepositioning Force and of the T-AGOS ocean surveillance classes, the only ships fitted to stream the great mile-long UQQ-2 SURTASS hydrophonic arrays that are becoming so important in ASW. Most MSC ships carry designations beginning with the letter 'T.'

The Ready Reserve Force is a special group of ships maintained within the 135-ship National Defense Reserve Fleet (not to be confused with the Navy Reserve Force made up largely of decommissioned combat types). Mostly cargo ships and tankers, these Ready Reserve ships are maintained in such a high state of readiness that on request of the Navy via the MSC they could be fully reactivated in between five and 20 days. Thus they occupy a kind of intermediate zone between ships that are on active duty and those that are in what is normally thought of as reserve. The Navy is placing considerable emphasis on building up this force and hopes to have 116 ships in the RRF by 1990.

Oilers and Tankers

Oilers, or AOs, differ from tankers in that they are able to give underway replensishment to Navy ships at sea, whereas tankers merely transport fuel from port to port. Somewhat confusingly, the Navy uses the term 'Replenishment Oiler' (AOR) to refer to a special type of oiler that can replenish ships at sea with significant quantities of both fuel and munitions. Perhaps even more confusing, there is still another type of ship called a Combat Support Ship, or AOE, that also replenishes with fuel and munitions underway. For the sake of clarity (?) we shall discuss AOEs under a separate heading.

The Navy's oilers are currently distributed about evenly between the auxiliary and MSC fleets, but the balance will probably shift increasingly to the MSC as the new T-AO 187 *Henry J Kaiser* class ships, at least 20 of which are planned, enter service.

The newest AOs in the auxiliary fleet are those of the *Cimmaron* class: AO 177 *Cimmaron*, AO 178 *Monongahela*, AO 179 *Merrimack*, AO 180 *Willamette* and AO 186 *Platte*. Built in the early 1980s, the 27,500-ton *Cimmarons* are designed primarily to replenish conventional aircraft carriers, which they can do twice (as well as refueling six to eight escort ships) per outing. As designed, they can carry 72,000 bbl of fuel oil and 48,000 bbl of aviation fuel, but their hulls are now being lengthened, and by 1991 their displacement will have risen to nearly 38,000 tons and their fuel-carrying capacity to a total of 183,000 bbl. Surprisingly, this conversion will reduce their present 20 kt speed by less than one kt. They are being armed with two Mk 15 Phalanx mounts and will be fitted with acoustic and electronic countermeasures gear.

The other AOs in the auxiliary fleet are two ancient survivors (AO 98 *Caloosahatchee* and AO 99 *Canisteo*) of the

World War II *Ashtabula* class. These unarmed 36,500-tonners can carry 143,000 bbl of fuel, as well as limited quantities of munitions and dry stores. Presumably it will not be much longer before they are consigned to the NRDF.

The auxiliary fleet also operates seven *Wichita* class AORs: AOR 1 *Wichita*, AOR 2 *Milwaukee*, AOR 3 *Kansas City*, AOR 4 *Savannah*, AOR 5 *Wabash*, AOR 6 *Kalamazoo* and AOR *Roanoke*. These 41,350-ton, 20-kt ships entered service between 1969 and 1976. They can carry 175,000 bbl of fuel, 600 tons of munitions and 575 tons of provisions. Their armament varies, but the most heavily armed (the last four units in the class) are fitted with one eight-tube Mk 29 Sea Sparrow launcher and two Mk 15 Phalanx mounts. They are all eventually to be fitted with Mk 23 Target Acquisition System fire-control radars.

The newest oilers in the MCS fleet are the *Henry J Kaisers* (T-AO 187 *Henry J Kaiser*, T-AO 188 *Joshua Humphreys*, T-AO 189 *John Lenthal*, T-AO 190 *Andrew J Higgens*, plus about 16 more), which began to enter service in 1986. These 40,700-ton 20-kt ships can carry 180,000 bbl of fuel, as well as dry goods and eight 20-foot provisions containers. They will be fitted with two Mk 15 Phalanx mounts and have a helicopter pad on the fantail.

Of Korean War vintage are the six (nearly unpronounceable) *Neosho* class oilers operated by the MSC: T-AO 143 *Neosho*, T-AO 144 *Mississinewa*, T-AO 145 *Hassayampa*, T-AO *Kawishwi*, T-AO *Truckee* and T-AO *Ponchatoula*. These are unarmed 36,840-ton ships that have a 20-kt top speed and can carry 180,000 bbl of fuel.

The remaining AOs in the MSC fleet are the five units of the *Mispillon* class (T-AO 105 *Mispillon*, T-AO 106 *Navasota*, T-AO 107 *Passumpsic*, T-AO 108 *Pawcatuck* and T-AO 105 *Waccamaw*) that date from World War II. They displace 35,090 tons, have a 16-kt top speed and can carry 107,000 bbl of fuel and some dry cargo. They are unarmed but have a helicopter pad on the forward deck. Until the early 1980s the MSC also operated two World War II-type *Cimmaron* class oilers, but these are now in the NRDF.

Intermediate between oilers and tankers is a group of 13 ships that the MSC calls transport oilers, or T-AOTs. For the most part these ships do not have a capacity to replenish under way or, if they do, are too old and slow. But the Navy is

considering giving the nine newest of these ships, those of the early 1970s *Sealift* class (T-AOT 168-176), underway replenishment capabilities. The *Sealifts* are 16-kt, 33,000-ton ships capable of carrying an impressive 225,154 bbl of fuel. The MSC operates the (unarmed) *Sealifts*, via a commercial contractor, on a 20-year charter.

The MSC operates 17 ordinary tankers, and there are currently five more in the Ready Reserve Force. The newest are the MSC's five *Paul Buck* class ships, which entered service in 1985-6. Displacing 39,624 tons and capable of carrying 240,000 bbl of fuel, they may eventually be designated as T-AOTs.

TOP: *The oiler AO 51 Ashtabula, class leader, now in reserve.*
ABOVE: *The replenishment oiler AOR 1* Wichita, *class leader.*
RIGHT: *The oiler AO 186* Platte *(Cimmaron class).*

The fast combat support ship AOE 4 Detroit (Sacramento class).

Combat Support Ships

The distinction between Combat Support Ships, or AOEs, and Replenishment Oilers, or AORs, is, at best subtle. Both are underway replenishment auxiliary types that carry fuel, munitions and dry stores, but whereas the main cargo of the AORs is fuel, in the AOEs the emphasis shifts somewhat more in the direction of ammunition and stores.

There is only one class of AOEs currently in service, the four-unit *Sacramento* class consisting of AOE 1 *Sacramento,* AOE 2 *Camden*, AEO 3 *Seattle* and AOE 4 *Detroit*. These 53,600-ton ships entered service in the late 1960s, and because of their 26-kt speed they are considered especially suitable for replenishing Battle Groups. They can carry 177,000 bbl of fuel, 2150 tons of ammunition and 750 tons of provisions. They are armed with one Mk 29 eight-tube Sea Sparrow launcher and two Mk 15 Phalanx mounts, and they have hangars and can carry two UH-46 helicopters. They are being given new ECM and chaff-dispensing gear and are also being fitted with stand-alone Mk 23 TAS AA fire-control systems.

Navy plans call for a follow-up class of four more AOEs that are to begin joining the fleet at the end of the 1980s. Probably to be called the *Supply* class, these will be modified *Sacramentos* with better armament – possibly RAM AA missiles in place of Sea Sparrows and two Mk 88 Bushmaster chain guns to supplement the two Phalanx gatlings. They will also be fitted to carry three helicopters. They are expected to be able to carry 156,000 bbl of fuel and a total of about 2450 tons of munitions and stores.

Ammunition Ships

Ammunition Ships, or AEs, are underway replenishment ships dedicated primarily to carrying munitions (*ie*, no fuel and limited dry stores). The auxiliary fleet now operates twelve such ships, and a thirteenth, T-AE 26 *Kilauea*, has been consigned to the MSC.

The principal auxiliary AE class is made up of seven ships of the *Kilauea* class, AE 27 *Butte*, AE 28 *Santa Barbara*, AE 29 *Mount Hood*, AE 32 *Flint*, AE 33 *Shasta*, AE 34 *Mount Baker* and AE 35 *Kiska*. All these entered service between 1968 and 1972. They can travel at 20 kt, displace nearly 20,000 tons and have a cargo capacity of about 6500 tons, which they can transfer quickly via the sophisticated FAST rapid-replenishment system. They are armed with four (two twin-mounted) Mk 33 3-in/50-cal DP guns or (AE 32-35) two Phalanx mounts. They have hangars aft and can carry two UH-46 helicopters.

The other AEs in the auxiliary fleet are veterans of the 1950s. The three units of the *Nitro* class, AE 23 *Nitro*, AE 24 *Pyro* and AE 25 *Haleakula*, displace 17,450 tons, can make 20 kt and are armed with four Mk 33 3-in/50-cal DP guns. The two units of the *Suribachi* class, AE 21 *Suribachi* and AE 22 *Mauna Kea*, displace 17,000 tons, can make 21 kt and are similarly armed with Mk 33s.

A new class of five AEs to replace the *Nitros* and *Suribachis* has been planned for the early 1990s. So far known only as AE 36-40, they will displace 22,790 tons and will carry about 6000 tons of ammo and stores. Their probable armament will consist of two Mk 15 Phalanx mounts and two Mk 88 Bushmaster chain guns, and they will carry one or two helicopters. Yet fiscal constraints have so far delayed the beginning of their construction and could ultimately cancel it.

ABOVE: *The ammunition ship AE 23* Nitro, *class leader.*
ABOVE RIGHT: *The combat stores ship AFS 3* Niagara Falls (Mars *class*).

Combat Stores Ships

Combat Stores Ships, or AFSs, are underway replenishment ships that are primarily dedicated to transferring stores other than fuel or munitions. The auxiliary fleet has seven such ships, and the MSC three.

The seven *Mars* class AFSs, all of which entered service in the auxiliary fleet between 1963 and 1970, are AFS 1 *Mars*, AFS 2 *Sylvania*, AFS 3 *Niagara Falls*, AFS 4 *White Plains*, AFS 5 *Concord*, AFS 6 *San Diego* and AFS 7 *San Jose*. They displace 16,070 tons, can make 20 kt and can carry about 7000 tons of cargo. Their M-shaped cargo masts can transfer a load to a receiving ship in about 90 seconds. Two of their five holds carry general spare parts, one carries aviation spare parts and one carries provisions. They are currently armed with four (two twin mounts) Mk 33 3-in/50-cal DP guns, but these are being replaced with two Mk 15 Phalanx mounts. They carry two UH-46 helicopters.

The three *Lyness* class AFSs operated by the MSC, T-AFS 8 *Sirius*, T-AFS 9 *Spica* and T-AFS 10 *Saturn*, were acquired from Great Britain in the early 1980s. Built in the 1960s, they displace 16,790 tons. They have four holds and a cargo-carrying capacity roughly the same as that of the *Mars* ships. They are unarmed.

Submarine Tenders

The auxiliary fleet currently operates 12 Submarine Tenders, with one in reserve (AS 12 *Sperry*). Of these, five are specifically intended to service SSBNs, and the remainder SSNs.

The SSBN tenders belong to the *Simon Lake* class (AS 33 *Simon Lake* and AS 34 *Canopus*), to the *Hunley* class (AS 31 *Hunley* and AS 32 *Holland*) and to the single-ship *Proteus* class (AS 19). The *Simon Lakes* and the *Hunleys* are ships of the early 1960s, but only *Lakes* are fully able to service Trident-carrying submarines. Both classes displace about 20,000 tons and are equipped with 30-ton cranes. The 21,000 ton *Proteus* was launched in the 1940s and was converted to tend SSBNs in 1960. Since she is not really capable of servicing the newest generations of SSBNs, she has been increasingly used of late as a general-purpose tender.

The five units of the *L Y Spear* class of SSN tenders are AS 36 *L Y Spear*, AS 37 *Dixon*, AS 39 *Emory S Land*, AS 40 *Frank Cable* and AS 41 *McKee*. The first two entered service in the early 1970s, and the remaining three between 1979 and 1981, with some resultant differences between the two groups, the principal being that AS 39-41 were specifically configured to tend the new *Los Angeles* class SSNs. The *Spears* displace between 22,560 and 23,490 tons and each can provide support to 12 submarines, with as many as four alongside at once. The only armed ships, AS 39-41, carry two 40-mm Mk 19 grenade launchers, but all have helicopter pads. The remaining active SSN tenders are the two ships of the *Fulton* class. AS 11 *Fulton* was laid down in 1939, and AS 18 *Orion* in 1941. Though these 12,215-ton ships have been modernized to support nuclear attack submarines, that they are still even in service is remarkable.

Destroyer Tenders

All nine of the Navy's active Destroyer Tenders, or ADs, are operated by the auxiliary fleet, with one more, AD *Everglades*, in reserve. They are divided into two classes, the elder of which has the distinction of containing the second oldest ship in commission in the Navy, AD 15 *Prairie*. (The oldest ship is the sailing frigate *Constitution*).

The six newer ADs, belonging to the *Samuel Gompers* class, are AD 37 *Samuel Gompers*, AD 38 *Puget Sound*, AD 41 *Yellowstone*, AD 42 *Acadia*, AD 43 *Cape Cod* and AD 44 *Shenandoah*. Since the first two units are constructions of the mid-1960s, and the other four entered service in the early 1980s, the class may be thought of as containing two distinct sub-classes, the newer sub-class (*ie*, AD 41-44) being specifically tailored to service *Kidd* and *Spruance* class destroyers and *Perry* class frigates. All of the ships can, in fact, provide generally good service to a wide variety of cruisers, destroyers and frigates, and they have fully equipped workshops for the maintenance and repair of electronic equipment and missiles. The *Gompers* ships displace between 22,250 and 22,500 tons, can make 20 kt and are fitted with two 30-ton cranes and two 3.5-ton travelling cranes. They are armed with two 40-mm grenade launchers and two or four Mk 67 20-mm AA guns. All have helicopter pads. Between 1980 and 1985 AD 38 *Puget Sound* served as flagship for the 6th Fleet and consequently is equipped with some exceptionally sophisticated communications gear.

The three antique ADs of the *Dixie* class, laid down between 1938 and 1942, are AD 15 *Prairie*, AD 18 *Sierra* and AD 19 *Yosemite*. Despite their age they have been extensively modernized and have well-equipped workshops to tend to the needs of guided missile escorts. The *Dixies* displace 17,190 tons and carry Mk 67 20-mm AA guns.

Cargo Ships and Transports

Whereas the bulk of the underway replenishment types are operated by the auxiliary fleet, virtually all cargo and trans-

ABOVE: *The destroyer tender AD 37 Samuel Gompers, class leader.*
LEFT: *The destroyer tender AD 19 Yosemite (Dixie class).*

16,360 ton T-AK 286 *Vega* and the 11,150-ton T-AK 280 *Furman* and T-AK 282 *Marshfield*. *Vega*, a former Moore-McCormack Lines vessel, has an ice-strengthened hull for arctic service and can carry vertically-stowed Trident missiles in her No 3 hold. *Marshfield* is similarly configured to carry 16 Poseidon missiles. These and other submarine stores, including fuel, would normally be transferred to submarine tenders in distant ports.

The MSC owns 10 vehicle cargo ships and charters four others. Of the designated ships, the eight belonging to the *Algol* class (T-AKR 287-294) are being converted to the self-explanatory roll-on/roll-off (Ro-Ro) capability and have been earmarked as Rapid Response vessels (*ie*, those that would be used to supply US troops in the earliest stages of a conflict). Capable of 33 kt, they are the fastest cargo ships in the Navy. They displace 55,355 tons and have a range of 12,200 nm. Eventually two *Algols* will be placed in the RRF, where they will join seven other ships that have been Ro-Ro configured.

Of the many classes of general cargo ships that are operated under charter by the MSC or are in the RRF, the three that make up the Maritime Prepositioning Force are perhaps especially worthy of mention. These are the five newly-constructed units of the *Lt John P Bobo* class, the five converted Maersk merchantmen that make up the *Cpl Louis J Hauge, Jr* class and the three converted Waterman merchantmen of the *Sgt Matej Kocak* class. Various combinations of these ships form the three Maritime Preopositioning Squadrons that are permanently deployed in forward areas: MPS-1 (four ships) in the Eastern Atlantic, MPS-2 (5 ships) based at Diego Garcia in the Indian Ocean and MPS-3 based at Guam and Tinian in the Western Pacific. In aggregate, each squadron has the capacity to supply the more than 15,000 men of a Marine Amphibious Brigade for 30 days.

Compared to the profusion of types and classes of cargo ships, the situation with respect to troop transports is simplicity itself. There are only two classes, both made up of converted passenger ships and both now in reserve. The four 22,575-ton ships of the *Admiral* class (AP 122-126) can carry about 1760 troops and a large quantity of dry cargo. The three 20,700-ton ships of the *General* class (AP 110, 117 and 119) can carry up to 3825 troops. Both classes first entered service in the mid-1940s.

port types belong to the MSC or to the RRF and NDRF.

There are several different kinds of cargo ships – stores ships, general cargo ships, vehicle cargo ships (with or without 'roll-on/roll-off' capabilities), cargo barge carriers and so on. Of these, some have been built specially for the Navy, some have been purchased by the Navy from commercial sources and some are simply under charter. Since there are in all about 40 individual classes of cargo ships, only a representative few can be mentioned here.

Navy-owned cargo ships that are operated by the MSC are given letter designations and hull numbers, but ships under charter are not. The two principal designated types are T-AKs, or general cargo ships, and T-AKRs, or vehicle cargo ships. As of 1987 the MSC had only three T-AKs in active service, the

Other Support Ships and Craft

This final, enormous 'other' category of Navy ships and craft includes a truly bewildering variety of vessels – everything from the presidential yacht *Sequoia* to floating pile drivers, from the *Midway* class aircraft carrier trainer AVT 16 *Lexington* to the incredible three-man research submarine DSV 4 *Sea Cliff* that can dive to depths of over 20,000 ft.

Included in the category are such large ships as the two ex-amphibious LPDs that are now the auxiliary command ships AGF 11 *Coronado* (*Austin* class) and AGF 3 *La Salle* (*Raleigh* class) and the four 16,245-ton repair ships of the *Vulcan* class (AR 5-8). Even larger are two converted merchant tankers that are now the 69,320-ton hospital ships T-AH 19 *Mercy* and T-AH 20 *Comfort*. And ranging in displacement from 11,860 tons to 24,000 tons are the sophisticated range instrumentation ships, or T-AGMs, used for tracking missile when they are being tested.

Within this 'other' category few, if any, ships are more important than the new 2285-ton ocean surveillance ships of the *Stalwart* class (T-AGOS 1-14, with five more planned) that can stream the long UQQ-2 SURTASS passive sonar arrays. These are the most sensitive ASW sensors in existence, and data from them is instantly relayed by satellite to ASW command centers ashore.

Other important types are salvage ships (ARSs), submarine rescue ships (ASRs), oceanographic research ships (T-AGORs), floating docks (AFDs) and so on down through the largest single class in the category – the 81 YTB-type large harbor tugs – to a multitude of ferrys, lighters, torpedo retrievers and other craft too numerous to mention. Few such types could lay much claim to glamor, and fewer still could the Navy do without.

TOP ROW L-R: *The experimental surface effect craft (a form of air-cushion vehicle) SES-200; the guided missile ship AVM 1* Norton Sound (Currituck *class); and the harbor tug YTB 813* Poughkeepsie.

BOTTOM ROW L-R: *The salvage ship AS 36* L Y Spear, *class leader, and the submarine rescue ship ASR 21* Pigeon, *class leader.*

AFTERWORD

On 12 February 1987 John F Lehman, Jr, announced his intention to resign as Secretary of the Navy. Since 1981 the indefatigable Lehman had been the principal architect of the Navy's post-Vietnam renaissance. Widely hailed as the 'father of the 600-ship Navy,' he had been a potent force in reshaping many of the Navy's fundamental strategic doctrines.

LEFT: *John F Lehman, Jr, the so-called 'father of the 600-ship Navy.'*

ABOVE: *CV 43* Coral Sea *will be the first of the present group of US carriers to be withdrawn from active service. She will become an auxiliary in 1992.*

His surprise announcement came at a time when the Reagan Administration, beset by the backlash of the Iran-Contra affair and facing a Congress now firmly in Democratic hands, had every reason to expect mounting political opposition to its defense policies. A sharp debate over the Administration's proposal to start long-lead funding of the two additional *Nimitz* class carriers for the late 1990s had already erupted, and, doubtless in an effort to head off Congressional criticism, the Administration had proposed in its FY 1988 budget to reduce the total of new naval construction by 33 percent under early projections. Thus Lehman's departure could be seen more as a symptom of the Reagan Administration's growing lack of control over naval policy than as a factor contributing to it.

Thanks to initiatives taken by the Administration during Lehman's tenure the nation seems assured of a powerful Navy through the first half of the 1990s. But what the state of the fleet will be by the year 2000 depends largely on decisions made or not made during the rest of the 1980s.

A good many of the Navy's requirements for the late 1990s are fairly obvious even now. For one thing, we know what ships will be nearing the end of their service lives. *Coral Sea*, for example, will already have been subtracted from the carrier fleet, and not only the status of her sister ship, *Midway*, but very possibly of the four ships of the *Forrestal* class (all built in the 1950s), will be in doubt. Should none of these ships be operative by the end of the 90s, and should no new construction have been undertaken in the meantime, the carrier fleet would then consist not of 15, but of 11 ships, four of which (*Kennedy* and the *Kitty Hawks*) will be well over the 30-year age considered maximum. In such a case the carrier fleet of the year 2000 would have three fewer ships than it has today. It was with this in mind that Secretary Weinberger made his criticized request for two additional *Nimitzes*.

To cite another example, in the guided-missile antiaircraft destroyer fleet the 23-ship *Adams* class and the 10-ship *Coontz* class will both reach block obsolescence in the 1990s. (The youngest of these vessels will be 38 years old in 2000; the oldest, 43.) The only other guided missile destroyers now in the Navy's inventory are the four ships of the *Kidd* class, built in the late 1970s. The Navy has therefore placed great emphasis on building a new class of DDGs, the *Arleigh Burkes*, five of which were supposed to be built each year beginning 1987. But 'fiscal constraints' have already reduced the planned rate of construction by 40 percent, to three a year, for the remainder of the 1980s, and even this cut-back program, which Secretary Weinberger has said 'will only aggravate the shortage of AAW ships in the 1990s,' is under fire from critics on Capitol Hill.

As with ships, so with planes. The rate at which planes have to be replaced under normal operating conditions averages about 330 a year. In 1986 329 new naval aircraft were procured, but only 271 were authorized for 1987, and the roughly similar number that was projected for 1988 will probably not be increased but may very well be reduced. Thus in quantitative terms naval air strength could go on declining at an annual rate of nearly 20 percent under what is needed just for replacement.

Then there is the problem of technological obsolescence. Even now it is clear that some weapons systems such as ASROC, SUBROC, the Sea Sparrow and the Mk 46 torpedo need replacements more capable of dealing with the kind of combat conditions that would almost certainly obtain in the 1990s. This may soon be true of the A-6 Intruder as well, for remarkable as the Intruder is, it is fundamentally a design of

the 1960s. By the end of the century it will have to compete not only with aircraft two generations younger, but with the new AA weapons developed to deal with them.

Other forms of technological obsolescence are harder to predict. In a general way we may be able to assume that quieter submarines will inevitably create a need for new and more sensitive ASW sensors or that aircraft stealth technology will doubtless create a need for better radars. But precisely when and in what forms other significant innovations will appear is unknowable. Yet from experience we can be sure both that they will appear and that they could easily make some existing technologies dangerously obsolete almost overnight.

With great effort and at appalling financial cost America has rebuilt the Navy from its nadir of the 1970s. But all this expense of energy and treasure could amount to little more than a temporary quick fix if the nation and its leaders were subsequently to prove unwilling to continue to pay the price of maintaining what has been bought so dearly.

In February 1987 the Reagan Administration proposed as Lehman's successor the then-Assistant Secretary of Defense for Reserve Affairs James H Webb, Jr. It is difficult to think of a more attractive choice for the next Secretary of the Navy than this Naval Academy graduate, Vietnam hero, critically-acclaimed novelist and proven administrator. But Webb and future secretaries will have no small task ahead of them. In fact, they will need all the enlightened help they can get from their presidents, Congresses and countrymen.

ABOVE: *Soviet* Alfa *class SSNs, the fastest and deepest-diving combat submarines in the world, symbolize the challenge the US Navy will face in the 1990s.*
FAR LEFT: *DDG 3* John King (Adams *class) was laid down 30 years ago.*
LEFT: *The Sea Sparrow missile is one of several weapons in the Navy's arsenal that badly needs to be replaced.*
RIGHT: *The nuclear powered CVN 68* Nimitz, *pride of the fleet.*

INDEX

AAW See antiaircraft warfare
Abraham Lincoln (CVN 72) 98, 99, 101
Acacia (AD 42) 182
Acme class 172
acoustical signature masking 144, 171, 177
Admiral class 183
Adroit (MSO 509) 172-73
Aegis system (missile control) 30, 74, 125, 131
Affray (MSO 511) 172-73
Aggressive class *171, 172, 173*
Ainsworth (FF 1090) 144
air cushion 172, *184. See also* landing craft
air wings (carrier-based) 16, 29, 44, 52, 99, 106, 107
aircraft: on amphibious ships 150; antisubmarine 27, *50,* 51, 53; attack 21, *48,* 48, *49, 51,* 51; cargo/ transport 54; electronic warfare *52,* 52, 54; fighters *17, 24,* 29 *43, 44, 44, 45, 46, 47, 51,* 54, 67; inventory 36 (projected 186); patrol 26, *53,* 53; photo- reconnaissance 54; range 18; refueling 17, 48, 101, 106; replacement 17-18, 29, 44, 47, 51, and proposals for 59; tankers *48, 51, 54,* 54; tilt-rotor 21, *53*; trainers 54, 107; V/STOL *51,* 51, 59, *150,* 150, 152, 153 *See also specific aircraft*; helicopters
aircraft carriers *See* carriers, aircraft
airlift 32
Alabama (SSBN 731) 82
Alamo (LSD 33) 159
Alaska (SSBN) 82 732
Albacore (AGSS 569) 91
Albert David (FF 1050) 146
Albuquerque (SSN 706) 88
Alexander Hamilton (SSBN 617) 83
Algol class 183
Alpha (SSN, Soviet) 24, *186*
Alywin (FF 1081) 144
America (CV 66) *11,* 104, *105*
ammunition ships 180, *181*
AMRAAM (missile) 29, 31, *69,* 69
Amphibious Command Information System 159
amphibious fleet *18,* 18, 21, 51, 54, *149-50, 152-155, 157-59,* 150-61; as aircraft carriers 153; hull construction (plastic 161) (steel 160); innovation/modernization 150; inventory 150-51; medical facilities 152; range 152, 154, 155, 159, 160; replacement 154, 155; speed 158, 159, 160, 161; vehicle parking 152, 156, 159
Anchorage (LSD 36) 156
Anchorage class 156, *157*
Andrew J Higgens (T-AO 190) 178
Anglo-French submarines 80. *See also* Great Britain
antiaircraft warfare 118, 126, 130
antiaircraft weapons, 29-31, *53, 63, 66,* 112, 118*n*, 136, 141
Antietam (CG 54) 126

Antisubmarine Master Plan and Investment Strategy 26
antisubmarine warfare 13, 24, 26-7, 29, 51, 53, 63, 126, 130, 134, 140, 141; locating devices/senors 26, 75; mines 71
Antrim (FFG 20) 142
Aquilia (PHM 4) 166
Archerfish (SSN 678) 90
Arctic: as potential war zone 40; cargo service in 183
Aries (PHM 5) 166
Arkansas (CGN 41) *120,* 120
Arleigh Burke (DDG 51) *131,* 132
Arleigh Burke class 30, 72, 74, 130, 131-132, 186
armor plating 106, 112, 131. *See also* Kevlar
arms limitation 6
Arthur W Radford (DD 968) 136
Ashtabula (AO 51) *178*
Ashtabula class 178
Aspro (SSN 648) 90
ASROC (rocket) *25,* 26, *63,* 63, 125, 131, 133, 136, 141, 143, 144, 146, 147
ASW *See* antisubmarine warfare
Atlanta (SSN 712) 88
Atlantic Fleet 6, 78, 83, 90, 91, 93, 95, 106, 122, 126, 127, 133, 136, 144, 146, 151, 153, 154, 156, 158, 159
Aubrey Fitch (FFG 34) 142
Augusta (SSN 710) 88
Austin (LPD 4) *157,* 159
Austin class *157,* 158, 159
auxiliary fleet 171, 177, 178, 180, 181, 182, 184
Avenger (MCM 1) 172
Avenger class 171, 172, 173

Backfire (TU-26, USSR) *41*
Badger (FF 1071) 144
Bagley (FF 1069) 144
Bainbridge (CGN 25) *2-3,* 124
Bainbridge class *124,* 124
Baltimore (SSN 704) 88
Barb (SSN 596) 91
Barbel (SS 580) *95*
Barbel Class 95
Barbey (FF 1088) 144
Barbour County (LST 1195) 158
Barney (DDG 6) 134
Barnstable County (LST 1197) 158
Batfish (SSN 681) 90
Baton Rouge (SSN 689) 88
Battle Groups 16, 26, 29, 31, 98, 114, 119, 180; complement 34; and zones of defense 29, 31
battleships 22, *111, 113, 114,* 112-14; advantages/usefulness 22, 112; hull construction 112-13
Belknap (CG 26) 126
Belknap class 72, 123, *126,* 126, 127
Belleau Wood (LHA 3) 153
Benjamin Franklin (SSBN 640) *83,* 83
Benjamin Franklin class 82-3
Benjamin Stoddert (DDG 22) 134
Bennington (CVS 20) 107
Bergall (SSN 667) 90
Berkeley (DDG 15) 134

Biddle (CG 34) 126
Billfish (SSN 676) 90
Birmingham (SSN 695) 88
Blakely (FF 1072) 144
Blue Ridge (LCC 19) *159,* 159
Blue Ridge class 159
Bluefish (SSN 675) 90
Bon Homme Richard (CV 31) 107
Boone (FFG 28) 142
Boston (SSN 703) 88
Boulder (LST 1190) 158
Bowen (FF 1079) 144
Bradley, Omar 18
Bradley, (FF 1041) 146
Bremerton (SSN 968) 88
Brewton (FF 1086) 144
Briscoe (DD 977) 136
Bristol County (LST 1198) 158
Bronco (OV-10) 54
Bronstein (FF 1037) 147
Bronstein class *147,* 147
Brooke (FFG 1) *143,* 143
Brooke class 141, 142-43, 146
Brumby (FF 1044) 146
Buchanan (DDG 14) 134
Buffalo (SSN 715) 88
Bunker Hill (CG 52) *63,* 126
Butte (AE 27) 180

California (CGN 36) *101, 117,* 122
California class 72, *122,* 122, 126
Callaghan (DDG 994) 133
Caloosahatchee (AO 98) *32,* 178
Camden (AOE 2) 180
Canisteo (AO 99) 178
Canopus (AS 34) 181
CAP *See* combat air patrol
Cape Cod (AD 43) 182
Capodanno (FF 1093) 144
CAPTOR (mine) 29, 71
Cardinal (MSH 1) *172,* 172
Cardinal class 171-72
cargo transportation 150, 152, 155, 158, 159, 160, 161, 183; masts 181; roll on/roll off capability 183
Carl Vinson (CVN 70) *44,* 99, *101,* 101
Caron, (DD 970) *136,* 136
Carr (FFG 52) 142
carriers, aircraft *14,* 18, 54, *97, 98, 101, 103, 104, 105, 107, 109,* 98-109; and atomic weapons 9; building 31; classification 17; conversion to/ modification of 22, 99; cost 98; decks, angled 107, 109; deployment 98, hangar accommodation 101 (*See also* catapults; elevators); hull construction/armor 106; inventory 90; reactors 99, 102; refueling *36,* 177; strategic use of 14-16; and USSR fleet 38. *See also* air wings
carriers, cargo 32
Casimir Pulaski (SSBN 633) 83
catapults 101, 102, 106
Cavalla (SSN 684) 90
Champion (MCM 4) 172
Chandler (DDG 996) *133,* 133
Charles F Adams (DDG 2) 72, *134,* 134, 186

Charles F Adams class 134
Charleston (LKA 113) 159
Charleston class 159
Chicago (SSN 721)
'choke points' 40
Cimmaron (AO 177)
Cimmaron class *177,* 177, *178*
Cincinnati (SSN 693) 88
City of Corpus Christi (SSN 705) 88
Clark (FFG 11) 142
Claude V Ricketts (DDG 5) 134
Cleveland (LPD 7) 159
Clifton Sprague (FFG 16) *140,* 142
Clover (FF 1098) 147
Coast Guard 72, 73
coastal operations 164, 173
Cochrane (DDG 21) 134
combat air patrol 29
Combat Stores Ships 181
Combat Support Ship *177, 178*
Comfort (T-AH 20) 184
command ships: amphibious *159,* 159; auxilliary fleet 184. *See also* national; tactical
Comte de Grasse (DD 974) 136
computer guidance 30, 31, 51, 53, 63, 88, 101, 106, 125, 131; of sonar 74; of torpedos 70
Concord (AFS 5) 181
Connole (FF 1056) 144
Conolly (DD 979) 136
Conquest (MSO 488) 173
Constant (MSO 427) 173
Constellation (CV 64) 104, *105,*
Constitution (sailing frigate) *6,* 182, 184
Continental Navy 6
Conyngham (DDG 17) *4-5,* 134
Cook (FF 1083) 144
Coontz (DDG 40) 133
Coontz class 72, *133,* 133, 186
Copeland (FFG 25) 142
Coral Sea (CV 43) 47, 98, 107, *109, 185*
Coronado (AGF 11) *159,* 159, 184
Cpl Louis J Hauge, Jr class 183
Corsair (A-7) 17, *51,* 51
Craft of Opportunity Program (COOP) 173
Crommelin (FFG 37) 142
cruise missiles 14, 61, 86
cruisers 57, 72, 74, *117-20, 122-27,* 118-127; damaged 126; designed for nuclear propulsion 124; hunter- killer 118; intra-class variations 125; modernization/modification 118, 120, 122, 123, 124, 126; nuclear-powered 118-24 (and reactors 120); superstructure construction 127
Crusader (RF-8) 54
Currituck class *184*
Curts (FFG 38) 142
Cushing (DD 985) 136

Dace (SSN 607) 91
Dahlgren (DDG 43) 133
Dale (CG 19) 127
Dallas (SSN 700) 88
Daniel Boone (SSBN 629) 83

Daniel Webster (SSBN 626) 83
Darter (SS 576) 95
Darter class 95
David R Ray (DD 971) 136
Davidson (FF 1045) 146
De Soto County class (LST) 159
De Wert (FFG 45) 142
Decatur class 136
Defender (MCM 2) 172
Denver (LPD 9) 159
Department of Defense *34*
depth charge *63*
Des Moines (CA 134) 118, 127
destroyers 30, 57, 72, 74, 118, 125, *129-31, 134, 136,* 130-36; age, problems of 130, 133; cost 131; hangars 136; hull design 136; modernization 134; non-missile 136
destroyer tenders 182, *183*
Detroit (AOE 4) *180,* 180
Dewey (DDG 45) 133
Deyo (DD 989) 136
Diver class *184*
Dixie class 182, *183*
Dixon (AS 37) 181
Dolphin (AGSS 555) *95,* 95
Dolphin class 95
Donald B Beary (FF 1085) 144
Downes (FF 1070) 144
Doyle (FFG 39) 142
Drum (SSN 677) 90
Dubuque (LPD 8) *157,* 159
Duluth (LPD 6) 159
Duncan (FFG 10) 142
Durham (LKA 114) 159
Dwight D Eisenhower (CVN 69) *36,* 99, *101,* 101

Eagle (F-15) 59
early warning system 29, 52
Edson (DD 946) 136
Edward McDonnell (FF 1043) 146
El Paso (LKA 117) 159
electronic warfare: aircraft *52,* 52, 54; sensors 75, 180 (integrated 125, 136)
elevators 101, 102, 106, 107, 120
Elliot (DD 967) *130,* 136
Elmer Montgomery (FF 1082) 144
Elrod (FFG 55) 142
Emory S Land (AS 39) 181
Engage (MSO 433) 173
England (CG 22) 127
Enhance (MS 437) 173
Enterprise (CVN 65) *98* , 98, 99, *101,* 102, *103*
Enterprise class 102
escort ships 26, 27, 30, 31, 109, 118-19, 130, 131, 136, 142, 144, 147; and 'high-threat' environment 140
Essex (LHD 2) 152
Essex/Hancock (CV) class 107, *109*
Esteem (MSO 438) 173
Estocin (FFG 15) 142
Ethan Allen class 82, 92
Everglades (AD 24) 182
Excel (MSO 439) 173
Exploit (MSO 440) 173

Exultant (MSO 441) 173

Fabrion (FFG 22) 142
Fairfax County (LST 1193) *149*, 158
Falcon (F-16) *69*
Fanning (FF 1076) 144
Farragut (DDG 37) 133
Fast Patrol Boats 167
Fearless (MSO 442) 173
Fidelity (MSO 443) 173
Fife (DD 991) 136
Finback (SSN 670) 90
fire control systems *13*, 114, 120, 131,
    134, 136, 146, 152, 180; radar fire
    control 30-31, 44, 46, 74, 88, 101,
    102, 104, 106, 144, 178; torpedo 91,
    92, 93
flagships 118, 126, 159, 182
Flasher (SSN 613) 91
Flatley (FFG 21) 142
Fletcher (DD 992) 136
Flint (AE 32) 180
Florida (SSBN 728) 82
Flying Fish (SSN 673) 90
Ford (FFG 54) 142
Forrest Sherman class 136
Forrestal (CV 59) 98, 106
Forrestal class 97, 104, 106
Fort Fisher (LSD 40) 156, *157*
Fort McHenry (LSD 43) 155
Fort Snelling (LSD 30) 159
Fortify (MSO 446) 173
'forward defense' strategy 40
Fox (CG 33) 126
Francis Hammond (FF 1067) 144
Francis Scott Key (SSBN 657) 83
Frank Cable (AS 40) 181
Frederick (LST 1184) 158
Fresno (LST 1182) 158
frigates 57, 72, 73, 118, 120, 122, 123,
    130, 134, *139, 140, 143-44, 146-47,*
    140-47; experimental 147; hull
    stabilizers 144, 146; modifications
    144
Fulton (AS 11) 181
Fulton class 181
funding 9, 31, 98, 113, 130, 131, 152, 164,
    180
Furman (T-AK 280) 183

Gallant (MSO 489) *171*, 173
Gallery (FFG 26) 142
Garcia (FF 1040) 146
Garcia class 142, *146*, 146
Gary (FFG 51) 142
Gato (SSN 615) 91
Gearing class 136
Gemini (PHM 6) 166
General class 183
George Bancroft (SSBN 643) 83
George C Marshall (SSBN 654) 83
George Philip (FFG 12) 142
George Washington (CVN 73) 98, 99,
    101
George Washington (ex-SSBN 598) 78
George Washington Carver (SSBN
    656) 83
Georgia (SSBN 729) *80*, 82
Germantown (LSD 42) 155

Goldsborough (DDG 20) 134
Gorshkov, Sergei 99
Gray (FF 1054) 144
Grayling (SSN 646) 90
Great Britain, Royal Navy 112
Greenling (SSN 614) 91
Greyhound (C-2) 54
Gridley (CG 21) *24*, *127*, 127
Groton (SSN 694) 88
Guadalcanal (LPH 7) 155
Guam (LPH 9) *18*, *154*, 155
Guardfish (SSN 612) *90*, 91
Guardian (MCM 5) 172
Guitarro (SSN 665) 90
guns 32, *72*, 72-3, 112, 114, 118, 120, 124,
    126, 131, 133, 136, 141, 146, 147,
    153, 155, 161; mount *31*;
    replacements 142; 3-inch 147, 158,
    159. *See also* Phalanx
Gurnard (SSN 662) 90

Haddo (SSN 604) 91
Haddock (SSN 621) 91
Haleakula (AE 25) 180
Halsey (CG 23) 127
Halyburton (FFG 40) 142
Hammerhead (SSN 663) *88*, 90
Hancock See Essex
hangars 101, 136, 180; telescoping 142
Harlan County (LST 1196) 158
HARM (missile) 65
Harold E Holt (FF 1074) 144
Harpoon (missile) 22, 24, 26, *31, 61,*
    61, *65*, 65, 88, 91, *114*, 123, 124,
    126, 127, 131, 133, 141, 144
Harrier (AV-8) 21, 22, *51*, 51, 59, *150*,
    152, 153, *154*
Harry E Yarnell (CG 17) 127
Harry W Hill (DD 986) 136
Hassayampa (T-AO 145) 178
Hawes (FFG 53) 142
Hawk (missile) 63
Hawkbill (SSN 666) 90
Hawkeye (E-2C) 29, *52*, 52, *98*, 107
Hayler (DD 993) 136
Helena (SSN 725) 88
helicopters 21, 56-9, *58*, 75, 114, 125,
    133, 136, 156, 178, 180;
    antisubmarine warfare 27, 130;
    assault 59, 154; cargo/troop
    carriers 58 (heavy-lift 150, 153);
    carrier-based *57*, 107, 109; cruiser-
    based 120; refueling *54; See also*
    elevators; hangars, *specific*
    helicopters
Hellfire (missile) 65
Henry B Wilson (DDG 7) 134
Henry Clay (SSBN 625) 83
Henry J Kaiser (T-AO 187) 178
Henry J Kaiser class 177, 178
Henry L Stimson (SSBN 655) 83
Henry M Jackson (SSBN 730) 82
Hepburn (FF 1055) 144
Hercules (C-130) *54*, 54
Hercules (PHM 2) *164*, 164, 166
Hermitage (LSD 34) 159
Hewitt (DD 966) 136
High Point (PCH 1) *167*
Hoel (DDG 13) 134

Holland (AS 32) 181
Honolulu (SSN 718) *87*, 88
Horne, (CG 30) *126*, 126
Hornet (CVS 12) 107
Hornet (F/A-18) *17*, 17, 18, 29, 44, *46*,
    46, 48, *65*, *67*, 107
hospital ships 184
Houston (SSN 713) 88
Hunley (AS 31) 181
Hunley class 181
hydrofoil patrol boats 73, 164, *165*;
    operation of mechanism 164
Hyman G Rickover (SSN 709) 88

Idaho (BB 42) *9*
Illusive (MSO 448) *173*, 173
Impervious (MSO 449) 173
Implicit (MSO 455) *169*, 173
Inchon (LHP 12) *149, 150*, 155
Independence (CV 62) 97, 106
Indian Ocean (Fleet in) 151
Indianapolis (SSN 697) 88
Inflict (MSO 456) 173
Ingersoll (DD 990) 136
Ingraham (FFG 61) 142
Intruder (A-6) 17, 18, *43*, 48, 52, 59, *65*,
    105, 186
Iowa (BB 61) *1, 22*, 22, *58, 72, 114*, 114
Iowa class 22, 72, 73, 112, 114
Iran, naval forces in 133
Iroquois (UH-1) 58
Ivan Rogov class (USSR) *39*
Iwo Jima (LPH 2) 155
Iwo Jima class 51, 109, 150, *154*, 154-55

Jack (SSN 605) 91
Jack Williams (FFG 24) 142
Jacksonville (SSN 699) 88
James K Polk (SSBN 645) 83
James Madison (SSBN 627) 83
James Monroe (SSBN 622) 83
Jarrett (FFG 33) 142
'Jeff B' *See* landing craft
Jesse L Brown (FF 1089) 144
Jesse L Taylor (FFG 50) 142
John A Moore (FFG 19) 142
John Adams (SSBN 620) 83
John C Marshall (SSN 611) 93
John F Kennedy (CV 67) *30, 104*, 104,
    126
John F Kennedy class 104, 185
John H Sides (FFG 14) 142
John Hancock (DD 981) 136
John King (DDG 3) 134
John Lenthal (T-AO 189) 178
John Rodgers (DD 983) 136
John T Hall (FFG 32) 142
John Young (DDG 973) 136
Johnson, Louis 9
Joseph Hewes (FF 1078) 144
Joseph Strauss (DDG 16) 124
Josephus Daniels (CG 27) 126
Joshua Humphreys (T-AO 188) 178
Jouett (CG 29) 126
Julius A Furer (FFG 6) 143
Juneau (LPD 10) 159

Kalamazoo (AOR 6) 178
Kalkring (FFG 42) *140*, 142

Kamehameha (SSBN 642) 83
Kansas City (AOR 3) 178
Kauffman (FFG 59) 142
Kawishwi (T-AO 146) 178
Kevlar armor plating 106, 120, 122, 123,
    133
Key West (SSN 722) 88
Kidd (DDG 993) *129*, 133
Kidd class 57, 72, 74, 130, *133*, 133, 136,
    182
Kiev class (USSR) *41*, 152
Kilauea (T-AE 26) 180
Kilauea class 180
King (DDG 41) 133
Kinkaid (DD 965) 136
Kirk (FF 1087) 144
Kiska (AE 35) 180
Kitty Hawk (CVN 63) *51, 58*, 104 *105*
Kitty Hawk class 98, 104, *105*, 185
Knox (FF 1042) 144
Knox class 72, 74, 140, 142, *144*, 144
Koelsh (FF 1049) *146*, 146

L Y Spear (AS 36) 181
La Jolla (SSN 701) 88
La Moure County (LST 1194) 158
La Salle (AGF 3) 159, 184
Lafayette (SSBN 616) 83
Lafayette class 60, 77, 78, 82-3
Lake Champlain (CG 57) 126
LAMPS-I *56*, 142, 144, 146
LAMPS-III 27, 56, *57*, 131, 136, 141, 152
landing craft 150, 154, 156-59, *160-61*,
    160-61; air-cushion (LCAC) *21*, 21,
    150, 152, 155, 158, 159, 160; 'Jeff B'
    21, 150; mechanized 160-61;
    tracked 161
Lang (FF 1060) 144
Lapon (SSN 661) 90
laser guidance 32
Lawrence (DDG 4) 134
LCAC *See* landing craft, air cushion
Leader (MSO 490) 173
Leahy (CG 16) 127
Leahy class 124, 126, *127*, 127
Leftwich (DD 984) 136
Lewis B Fuller (FFG 23) 142
Lewis and Clark (SSBN 644) 83
Lexington (CV/AVT 16) 107, 184
Leyte Gulf (CG 55) 126
Light Airbourne Multi-Purpose System
    (LAMPS) 56. *See also* LAMPS
Lockwood (FF 1064) 144
Long Beach (CGN 9) *119, 124*, 124-5
Long Beach class 124
Los Angeles (SSN 688) 91
Los Angeles class 24, 63, *71*, 74, *86*, 86,
    87, 87-8, 181
Louisville (SSN 724) 88
Luce (DDG 38) 133
Lynde McCormick (DDG 8) 134
Lyness class 181

MacArthur, Douglas 18
McCandless (FF 1084) 144
McCloy (FF 1038) *147*, 147
McClusky (FFG 41) 142
Macdonough (DDG 39) 133

McInerney (FFG 8) 142
McKee (AS 41) 181
McNamara, Robert 122
magnetic anomaly detectors 51, 53, *75*,
    75
magnetic mines 58, 71
Mahan (DDG 42) 133
Mahlon S Tisdale (FFG 27) 142
Manitowoc (LST 1180) 158
Mariano G Vallejo (SSBN 658) 83
Marines: air wings 44, 48, 51;
    amphibious forces 18, 22, 32, 34-5,
    54, 150, 183
Maritime Prepositioning Force 21-2,
    22, 151, 177, 183
Mars (AFS 1) 181
Mars class 181
Marshfield (T-AK 282) 183
Marvin Shields (FF 1066) *144*, 144
Mauna Kea (AE 22) 180
Maverick (missile) *65*
Mediterranean Fleet 114, 151
Memphis (SSN 691) 88
Mendel Rivers (SSN 686) 90
merchant marine 32
Mercy (T-AH 19) 184
Merrimack (AO 179) 177
Merrill (DD 976) 136
Meyerkord (FF 1058) 144
Michigan (SSBN 727) *60*, 82
Midway (CV 41) *43*, 47, *98*, 98, *107*,
    107
Military Sealift Command 32, 177, 178,
    180
Miller (FF 1091) 144
Milwaukee (AOR 2)
Mine Neutralization System 171-72
minelayers 71, 167
mines 29, 39, *71*, 71, 86;
    countermeasures 75, 170-73;
    torpedo-launched 71
minesweepers/hunters 58, *169*, 170-73,
    172; conversion to 173; hull
    construction 171, 172; *See also* Sea
    Stallion RH-53
Minneapolis-Saint Paul (SSN 708) 88
Mispillon (T-AO 105) *177*, 178
Mispillon class 178
missiles: air-to-air 29, 31, 44, 66, 69; air-
    to-surface 17, *65*, 65; anti-tank 65;
    antisubmarine 63; ballistic 60;
    cruiser-based, first 124; homing
    30; interception of 13; launchers
    72, 101, 124, 133, 141, 142;
    platforms 113, 120; range
    differentiation 14; replacements
    31, 60, 62; ship-to-ship 22; surface-
    to-air 29, 62-3, 130; surface-to-
    surface 61; tracking 184; vertical
    launch system 88, 136.
See also cruise missiles; *specific*
    missiles
missions, naval: deterrence 12-13;
    power projection 14-17, 18, 21, 22;
    sea control 22, 26, 31-2; transport
    32
Mississinewa (T-AO 144) 178
Mississippi (CGN 40) *120*, 120
Missouri (BB 63) 22, 112, *113, 114*, 114

Mobile (LKA 115) 159
Mobile Bay (CG 53) 126
Moinester (FF 1097) 144
Monongabela (AO 178) *177*, 177
Monticello (LSD 35) 159
Moosbrugger (DD 980) 136
Mount Baker (AE 34) 180
Mount Hood (AE 29) 180
Mount Vernon (LSD 39) 156
Mount Whitney (LCC 20) 159

Nashville (LPD 13) 159
Nassau (LHA 4) *150, 153,* 153
Nathanael Greene (SSBN 636) 83
national command ship 118
National Defense Reserve Fleet 159, 177
NATO 32; fleet 39, 171; and /US strategy 40. See also Anglo-French
Nautilus (SSN 571) *24,* 24, 80
Naval Intelligence Processing System 159
Naval Reserve Forces See reserve fleet
Navasola (T-AO 106) 178
Nebraska (SSBN 733) 82
Neosho (T-AO 143) *175,* 178
Neosho class 178
New Jersey (BB 62) 22, *111,* 112, *113, 114*
New Orleans (LPH 11) 155
New Threat Upgrade 126, 133
New York City (SSN 969) 88
Newport (LST 1179) 158
Newport class 158-59, *159*
Newport News (SSN 750) 88
Niagara Falls (AFS 3) *181,* 181
Nicholas (FFG 47) 142
Nicholson (DD 982) 136
Nimitz (CVN 68) *14,* 98, 99, 101, *186*
Nimitz class 99-101
Nitro (AE 23) 180, *181*
Nitro class 180
Norfolk (SSN 714) 88, 118
Northampton (CLC/CC 1) 118
Norton Sound (AVM 1) *184*
nuclear reactors 80, 88, 90, 92, 93, 99, 102, 120, and cruiser design 124

O'Bannon (DD 987) 136
O'Brien (DD975) 136
O'Callaban (FF 1051) 146
Ogden (LPD 5) 159
Ohio (SSBN 726) *79, 80,* 80
Ohio class *13,* 60, 74, 78, 80-2, 83
oilers *175,* 177-78, *178*; replenishment 177, 180; transport 178
Oklahoma City (SSN 723) 88
Okinawa (LPH 3) 155
Oldendorf (DD 972) 136
Oliver Hazard Perry (FFG 7) *139, 140,* 142
Oliver Hazard Perry class 57, 73, *140,* 140, 141-42, *143*
Olympia (SSN 717) 88
Omaha (SSN 692) 88
Orion (P-3) *27, 53,* 53, *71*
Orion (AS 18) 181
Oriskany (CV 34) 107
Osprey (MV-22) 21, *53,* 54, 150

Ouellet (FF 1077) 144

Pacific Fleet 78, 90, 91, 95, 102, 106, 122, 123, 124, 126, 127, 133, 136, 144, 146, 151, 153, 154, 156, 159
parachute-launched torpedos 63
Parche (SSN 683) 90
Pargo (SSN 650) *70,* 90
Passumpsic (T-AO 107) 178
Patterson (FF 1061) 144
Paul (FF 1080) 144
Paul Buck class 178
Paul K Forster (DD 964) 136
Pawcatuck (T-AI 108) 178
Pegasus (PHM 1) *164,* 164, 166
Pegasus class 73, *163*
Peleliu (LHA 5) 153
Penguin II (missile) 65, 166
Pensacola (LSD 38) 156
Peoria (LST 1183) 159
Permit (SSN 594) 91
Permit class 61, 63, 89, *90,* 91
Peterson (DD 969) 146
Phalanx (gun) *30,* 30, 31, *73,* 73, 101, 102, 104, 106, 107, 123, 124, 127, 133, 134, 136, 141, 144, 152, 154, 155, 156, 158, 158, 159, 177, 178, 180
Phantom (F-4) *43, 47,* 47, 109
Pharris (FF 1094) 144
Philadelphia (SSN 690) 88
Phoenix (SSN 702) 88
Phoenix (missile) 29, 44, *69,* 69
Pigeon (ASR 21) *184*
Pintado (SSN 672) 90
Pittsburgh (SSN 720) 88
Platte (AO 186) 177, *178*
Pledge (MSO 492) 173
Pluck (MSO 464) 173
Plunger (SSN 595) 91
Plymouth Rock (LSD 29) 159
Pogy (SSN 647) 90
Point Defiance (LSD 31) 159
Polaris (missile) 82, 124
Pollack (SSN 603) 91
Ponce (LPD 15) 159
Ponchatoula (T-AO 148) 178
pontoon causeways 158
Portland (LSD 37) 156
Portsmouth (SSN 707) 88
Poseidon (missile) 60, *60,* 78, 82, 183
Poughkeepsie (YTB 818) *184*
Powatan (T-AFT 166) *177*
Prairie (AD 15) 182
Prairie-Masker bubble system 144
Preble (DDG 46) *133,* 133
Precision Integrated Navigation System 171, 172
Preserver (ARS 8) *184*
propulsion 160; gas turbine 136; propellor 95, 147; standard 91, 92, 144; waterjet *164,* 166, 167. See also nuclear reactors
Providence (SSN 719) 88
Prowler (EA-6) *16, 52,* 52, 75, 107
Puffer (SSN 652) 90
Puget Sound (AD 38) 182

Pyro (AE 24) 180

Queenfish (SSN 651) 90
Quickstrike (mine) 29, 71

Racine (LST 1191) 158
radar 29, 48, 52, 62, 102, *103,* 104, 125, 144, 159, 160; air-search *74,* 74, 101, 104, 120 and infrared 31, 53; and anti-radar missile 65, 66 replacement 122, 134; surface-search 114, 152; synthetic aperture 51. See also fire control
Raleigh (LPD 1) 158
Raleigh class *158,* 158, 159
RAM (missile) 31, 63, 101
Ramsey (FFG 2) 143
Ranger (CV 62) *48, 106,* 106
Rapid Deployment Strategy 32
Rapid Response vessels 183
Rathburn (FF 1057) 144
Ray (SSN 653) 90
Ready Reserve 32, 48, 151, 177, 178
Reasoner (FF 1063) 144
Reeves (CG 24) 127
Reid (FFG 30) 142
Regulus II (missile) 124
Rentz (FFG 6) 142
repair ships 184
research, oceanographic 184
reserve fleet 92, 118, 127, 144, 146, 155, 158, 159, 164, 167, 171, 177
retirement (of ships) 36, 78, 83, 92, 98, 112, 136, 159; and reactivation 98, 112, 113-14, 159
Reuben James (FFG 57) 142
Richard B Russell (SNN 687) 90
Richard E Byrd (DDG 23) 134
Richard L Page (FFG 5) 143
Richmond K Turner (CG 20) 127
Roanoke (AOR 7) 178
Roark (FF 1053) 144
Robert E Beadley (FFG 49) 142
Robert E Peary (FF 1073) 144
Robinson (DDG 12) 134
rockets: antisubmarine 26, 88; See also ASROC; SUBROC
Rodney M Davis (FFG 60) 142
RoRo See cargo

Sacramento (AOE 1) 180
Sacramento class 180
Saginaw (LST 2288) 158
St Louis (LKA 116) 159
Saipan (LHA 2) 153
Salem (CA 139) 127
Salt Lake City (SSN 716) 88
SALT II treaty 83
salvage ships *184,* 184
Sam Houston (SSN 609) 93
SAM see missiles: surface-to-air
Sample (FF 1048) 146
Sampson (DDG 10) 134
Samuel B Roberts (FFG 58) 142
Samuel Eliot Morison (FFG 13) 142
Samuel Gompers (AD 37) 182, *183*
Samuel Gompers class 182
San Bernardino (LST 1189) 158
San Diego (AFS 6) 181

San Jacinto (CG 56) 125
San Jose (AFS 7) 181
San Francisco (SSN 711) 88
San Juan (SSN 751) 88
Sandlace (SSN 660) 90
Santa Barbara (AE 28) 180
Saratoga (CV 60) 98, 106
Sargo (SSN 583) 93
satellite communications 26, 88, 114, 159, 184
Saturn (T-AFS 10) 181
Savannah (AOR 4) *177,* 178
Scamp (SSN 588) 92, *93*
Schofield (FFG 3) 143
Scorpion (SSN 589) 92
Scott (DDG 995) 133
Sculpin (SSN 591) 92
Sea Cobra (AH-1) 59
Sea Devil (SSN 664) 90
Sea Dragon (MH-53) 58
Sea King (SH-3) *56,* 56, *70,* 75, 107
Sea Knight (CH-46) *21,* 21, *58,* 58, *114,* 152, 153, 154, 159
Sea Lance (missile) 26, 63
Sea Sparrow (missile) *30,* 30, 62, *63,* 101, 102, 104, 106, 107, 136, 144, 152, 153, 154, 180, *186*
'Sea Spectre' class *165,* 166
Sea Stallion (CH-53) *54,* 58, 155; RH-53 154, *171*
'Seafox' class 167
Seahawk (SH-60B) *27,* 27, 56-7, *57,* 125
Seahorse (SSN 669) 90
SEAL (Sea, Air, Land Teams) 164, 166, 167
Sea Lance (rocket) 63, 88
sealift 32
Sealift class 178
Seasprite (SH-2) *56,* 56, 75, 125
Seattle (AOE 3) 180
Seawolf (SSN 21) *24, 85,* 86
Seawolf class 26, 40, 63, 86-7
Second Fleet 34
Second Lt John H Bobo 22
Second Lt John H Bobo class 183
Sellers (DDG 11) 134
Semmes (DDG 18) 134
sensors 26, 48, 51, 74-5, 171
Sentry (MCM 3) 172
Sgt Matej Kocak class 183
Service Life Extension Program (SLEP) 98, 104, 106, 156, 158, 159
Seventh Fleet 34
Shark (SSN 591) 92
Shasta (AE 33) 180
Shenandoah (AD 44) 182
Shreveport (LPD 12) 159
Shrike (missile) 65
Sidearm (missile) 66
Sidewinder (missile) 29, *66,* 66, 67
Sierra (AD 18) 182
Silversides (SSN 679) 90
Simon Bolivar (SSBN 641) 83
Simon Lake (AS 33) 181
Simon Lake class 181
Simpson (FFG 56) 142
Sirius (T-AFS 8) 181
Sixth Fleet 34
Skate class *93,* 93

Skipjack (SSN 585) *91*
Skipjack class 91-2
Skipper (missile) *65,* 65
Skyhawk (A-4) *48,* 48
Skywarrior (EA-3) 54
SLMM (mine) 29
SM-1/2 missiles See Standard
Snook (SSN 592) 92
sonar 26, 74-7, 88, 90, 91, 92, 101, 120, 122, 125, 131, 133, 136, 144, 146; digital 91; dipping 57, *75,* 75; mine-hunting 171, 172; under-ice 74, 88; See also STASS, SUBACS, SURTASS, TACTASS
sonobuoys 26, 75
Sound Surveillance System (SOSUS) 26, 75
South Carolina (CGN 37) *122,* 122
Soviets See USSR
Spadefish (SSN 668) 90
Sparrow (missile) 29, *66,* 66
Spartanburg County (LST 1192) 158
Special Warfare Craft 166-67
Sperry (AS 12) 181
Spica (T-AFS 9) 181
Spiegel Grove (LSD 32) *150, 157,* 159
Springfield (SSN 752) 88
Spruance (DD 963) *136,* 136
Spruance class 72, *74,* 74, 125, *130,* 130, 136, 182
SPY-1 (radar) 30, *74,* 74, 101, 102, 104, 125, 131
Stalwart class 184
Standard (missile) *29,* 29-30, 62-3, 120, 123, 124, 126, 127, 131, 133
Stark (FFG 31) 142
STASS (sonar) 74
Stein (FF 1065) *144,* 144
Stephen W Groves (FFG 29) 142
Sterett (CG 31) 126
Stonewall Jackson (SSBN 634) 83
Strategic Defense Initiative 36
Stump (DD 978) 136
Sturgeon (SSN 637) 90
Sturgeon class *88,* 88, 89-90, 93
SUBACS (sonar system) 74, 88
submarines: circumnavigation 88; conventional 95; deterrent patrols 78, 80; diesel 37, 86; hull construction 82, 95; missile capacity 13; propulsion (conventional) 95; quietness 95; research *95,* 95, 184; rescue 184; robot 171; size *24;* sonars 74, 88; torpedo capacity 22, 95
submarines, nuclear-powered attack *13,* 22, 24, 26, *85, 86,* 86-93; crew 93; diving capability 91; hull design 91; inventory 86; lost 91, 92; maneuverability 87; modifications/conversions 89-90, 92; propulsion (standard) 91, 92; quietness 91; reactors 88, 90, 92, 93; speed 93; in USSR fleet 38-9, 87-8; and US/USSR strategy 40-1; under-ice capability 89, 93
submarines, strategic missile 78-83; building 78; crews 78, 83; quietness of 80, 82; reactors 80

submarine tenders 181
SUBROC (rocket) 24, 63, 88
Suffolk County (LST 1173) *150*
Sumner class 136
Sumpter (LST 1181) 158
Sunfish (SSN 649) 90
Super Cobra (AH-1) 59
Super Stallion (CH-53E) 21, *58*, 58, 150
Supply class 180
support ships 177-84; armament 178,
    180, 181, 182; cargo capacity 180;
    combat *180*; commands
    administering 177; conversion
    177, 183; replacements 180; speed
    180, 183
Surface Action Group 22, 26, 31, 114
Suribachi (AE 21) 180
SURTASS (Sonar) 177, 184
surveillance 177, 184
Swath class 184
'Swift' class 167
Swordfish (SSN 579) *93*, 93
Sylvania (AFS 2) 181

TACTAS (sonar) 74, 133
tactical command ships 118
Tactical Data System 144
Tactical Flag Communications Center
    102, 106
Talbot (FFG 4) 143
tankers *See* oilers
Tarawa (LHA 1) *18*, 153
Tarawa class 51, 109, 150, 152-53, *153*
Target Recognition-Attack Multisensor
    System 48
Tatnal (DDG 19) 134
Taurus (PHM 3) 166
Tautog (SSN 639) 90
Tecumseh (SSBN 628) 83
Tennessee (SSBN 734) 82
Terrebonne County (LST) class 159
Terrier (missiles) 126
Texas (CGN 39) 120
Thach (FFG 43) 142
Theodore Roosevelt (CVN 71) 98, 99,
    101, 106
Third Fleet 34
Thomas A Edison (SSBN 610) 92
Thomas C Hart (FF 1092) 144
Thomas G Gates) (CG 51) 126
Thomas Jefferson (SSBN 618) 92
Thomaston (LSD 28) 159
Thomaston class 155, 156, *157*
Thorn (DD 988) 136
Ticonderoga (CG 47) *72, 74, 118*, 126
Ticonderoga class 30, 57, 63, 72, 74,
    119, *125*, 125-6, 131, 136
Tinosa (SSN 606) 91
Tomahawk (missile) *14*, 14, 22, 24, 26,
    61, 61, 86, 88, 90, 131, 136;
    launchers 114, 120, 122, 124
Tomcat (F-14) 18, *29*, 29, *44*, 44, 59,
    69, 69
torpedos 24, 26, 70; Mk 46 *26*-7, 29, *70*,
    131; Mk 48 22, *70*;
    launching systems 26-7, 63, 70, 89,
    123; replacement 27; and SSNs
    86,87
Towed Array Sonar Systems 26, 74, 90,

125, 131, 136, 141, 144, 146, 147
Towers (DDG 9) 134
training ships 54, 107, 112, 136, 173, 184
Trepang (SSN 674) 90
Trenton (LPD 14) 158
Trident (missile) *15, 79*, 183; C-4 13,
    60, 60, 78, 80, 82; D-5 13, 41, 60
Tripoli (LPH 10) *154*, 155
Trippe (FF 1075) 144
troop transport 21, 54, 150, 152, 155,
    156, 158, 159, 160, 161, 183
Truckee (T-AO 147) 178
Truett (FF 1095) 144
Truxton (CGN 35) *123*, 123, 126
Truxton class 72, 123
tugs *177*
Tullabee (SSN 597) 93
Tunny (SSN 682) 90
Tuscaloosa (LST 1185) 158
Typhoon class (USSR) *40*, 78

Ulysses S Grant (SSBN 631) 77, 83
Underwood (FFG 36) 142
United States Congress, and ship
    classification 123 *See also* funding;
    ship construction *below*
United States Military: Command
    organization 34; Department of
    Defense STRAT-X study 80
United States Navy: air force 44 (*See
    also* air wings); classification of
    ships 118, 120, 123, 125, 126, 127,
    133, 140; development of 6; Fleet
    organization 34, *35*; personnel
    and inventory 35, 36; size
    (projected/proposed 18, 131, 151,
    155, 164, 166, 173, 180, 184, 185-86
    and new ship construction 36, 86,
    98, 118, 119, 122, 130, 140, 141, 154,
    164) (Vietnam War/ and post – 9,
    18, 112) (in World War II 9);
    strategy/policy 26, 32, 40-1, 78, 118,
    130, 170-71, 185-86. *See also*
    funding; missions; Ready Reserve;
    Secretary of the Navy
USSR, Naval forces 9, *35*, 38-40, *39, 40,
    41*, 78, 86, 99, 152, *186*

Valdez (FF 1096) 144
Valley Forge (CG 50) 126
Vancouver (LPD 2) *158*, 158
Vandegrift (FFG 48) 142
Vega (T-AK 286) 183
vertical launch system *See* missiles
Vertical/Short Take-Off and Landing
    aircraft (V/STOL) 59, 98-9, 109,
    113, 125, 150
Victor (USSR) 87
Viking (S-3) *27*, 27, *51*, 51
Vincennes (CG 49) *63*, 126
Virginia (CGN 38) 120
Virginia class 72, *120*, 120, 122
Voge (FF 1047) 146
Von Steuben (SSBN 632) 83
Vreeland (FF 1068) 144
Vulcan class 184

Wabash (AOR 5) 178
Waccamaw (T-AO 109) 178

Waddell (DDG 24) 134
Wadsworth (FFG 9) 142
Wainwright (CG 28) 126
Wasp (LHD 1) *152*, 152
Wasp class ships 21, 22, 51, 109, 150,
    151, 152, 154
Watkins, James *36*
weapons 60-73; air defense 73;
    antiaircraft 29-31; obsolescence
    186; upgrade program 126, 133
Weinberger, Caspar 98, 130, 186
Whale (SSN 638) 89
Whidbey Island (LSD 41) *155*, 155
Whidbey Island class 150, 151, 155
Whipple (FF 1062) 144
White Plains (AFS 4) 181
Wichita (AOR 1) *178*, 178
Wichita class 178
Will Rogers (SSBN 659) 83
Willamette (AO 180) 177
William H Bates (SSN 680) 90
William S Sims (FF 1059) 144
William Standley (CG 32) 126
William V Pratt (DDG 44) 133
Wisconsin (BB 64) 22, 114
Woodrow Wilson (SSBN 624) 83
Worden (CG 18) 127

Yorktown (CG 48) 126
Yosemite (AD 19) 182, *183*

Zumwalt, Elmo, Jr 164

Acknowledgments

The publisher would like to thank the following individuals who helped in the preparation of this book; Mike Rose, who designed it; John Kirk, who edited it; Jean Chiaramonte Martin, who did the picture research; and Cynthia Klein, who prepared the index. Special thanks go to the US Navy for supplying all the illustrations except for the following:

Bison Picture Library: pages 7, 51, 98 (top).
Richard Natkiel (maps): pages 35, 39.
Sikorsky: pages 57, 171.
US Marines: page 161 (bottom).
© Bill Yenne: page 65 (left).